PUSHING BACK THE

INVASION

FROM THE KINGDOM OF DARKNESS

KNOWING HOW TO EXERCISE DOMINION OVER EVIL SPIRITS

MUSA BAKO

Printed in the United States of America.

ISBN   Paperback   979-8-32657-743-6

Boundless Script Ventures
99 Wall Street #210
New York, NY, 10005

www.boundlessscript.com

To all the soldiers of Jesus, in all nations, who are fighting the good fight of faith, pushing back the darkness, shining the light of the gospel, and enthroning Jesus in their sphere of influence.

Receive God's grace to shine even brighter. Amen!

CONTENTS

PROLOGUE

THE INVASION FROM DARKNESS

Satan wants to be a god in the hearts of all people and in all nations, and he seeks control over communities, villages, towns, and cities. He seeks to rule over all institutions of learning and leaders of governments of nations. He wants to control all people and all creation and be like the Most High God, which is a position he has long coveted. Satan even aspires to place his throne elevated and above the stars of God. The writer of the book of Isaiah puts it this way:

> "How you have fallen from heaven, morning star, son of the dawn! You have been cast down to the earth, you who once laid low the nations! [13] You said in your heart, "I will ascend to the heavens; I will raise my throne above the stars of God; I will sit enthroned on the mount of assembly, on the utmost heights of Mount Zaphon. [14] I will ascend above the tops of the clouds; I will make myself like the Most High" (Isaiah 14:12-16 KJV).

The mount of assembly, perched atop the lofty heights of Mount Zaphon, where Satan presumed to sit enthroned, coincides precisely with the very place where God resides and reigns. It is the spiritual place where both angels and humans who are saved are spiritually assembled. This is revealed to us in the book of Hebrews, which reads:

> "But ye are come unto mount Sion, and unto the city of the living God, the heavenly Jerusalem, and to an innumerable company of angels, [23] To the general assembly and church of the firstborn, which are written in heaven, and to God the Judge of all, and to the spirits of just men made perfect (Hebrews 12:22-23 KJV).

If Satan had succeeded in his treason against God and ascended on the mount of the assembly, as he had coveted, and was enthroned above the stars of God, he would have had the rule over God, over all angelic beings, and over the saints of God. However, Lucifer, who is now Satan the devil, was rejected by God for his effrontery, stripped of his elevated position among angels, and cast out of heaven. However, he succeeded in taking down with him a third of the angels who aligned with him in his rebellion against God. These rebellious fallen angels are the spirits we refer to as demons or evil spirits. (I will be interchanging demons and evil spirits throughout this book, and Satan and the devil; note that they are the same beings.) There are millions, even tens of millions, of fallen demons—a substantial number, constituting a third of all the angels.

Satan is the god of this present world system, and he seeks to permeate every aspect of the human experience and rule in it. He has organised his fallen angels, the evil spirits, into various orders, cadres, and hierarchies, and they all function in different areas of assignment. Evil spirits operate in various categories of assignments, and each category is responsible for a particular kind of behavioural disorder that we see in humans. For example, there are demons responsible for immorality and perversion; these spirits are also called unclean spirits (Luke 4:33). There are demons of infirmity; these demons are responsible for all manner of illnesses and diseases in people (Luke 13:11). There are demons of bondage; they steal people's destiny and subject them to all kinds of misery and cruelty (Roman 8:15). Demons of bondage are the evil spirits behind fear. Fear is designed to hold people under bondage and to inhibit their ability to live to their full potential.

Demons are unleashed everywhere in the world, and they are creating all kinds of problems for humanity. They are responsible for drunkenness, drug addictions, crime and violence, horrible deaths, murder, suicide etc. In most cases, the demon that is in operation in any area can be identified by looking at the prevalent, ungodly activities being witnessed in the place. You can also tell what spirit is operating in someone by looking at their behaviour, the lifestyle in which they live or the problems they are experiencing. There is the story of someone in the Bible who was deaf and dumb; he was deaf and dumb because he was possessed by a deaf and dumb spirit. However, he was made whole and could hear and speak after Jesus cast out the deaf and dumb spirit from him.

> "When Jesus saw that a crowd was running to the scene, he rebuked the impure spirit. "You deaf and mute spirit," he said, "I command you, come out of him and never enter him again." [26] The spirit

shrieked, convulsed him violently and came out. The boy looked so much like a corpse that many said, "He's dead." [27] But Jesus took him by the hand and lifted him to his feet, and he stood up" (Mark 9:25-27 NIV).

Irrespective of any demon's hierarchy or their assignment, the demon's major target is to bring all human beings under subjugation and to make Satan a god. In pursuit of this, they seek to make those who are believers in Christ Jesus work away from their faith in Jesus or to ruin their purpose and calling. As a believer, you must always be aware that there are millions of demons out there in our world, sent by Satan to fight believers, to overthrow their faith, and to destroy their purpose and calling. These demons will not relent until the second coming of Jesus or the exit of a believer from the earth at his death. Don't forget, the fundamental drive of all evil spirits is to destroy God's purpose behind the creation of man and enthrone Satan as a god, thereby undermining God.

Evil spirits use all sorts of schemes to achieve their assignments. They subtly creep into churches, introducing false teachings and doctrines, to get believers to deviate from the truth of the gospel, thereby embracing satanic ideologies and doctrines and paving the way for demons to have control. This is why John the Apostle admonishes believers, saying:

> "Beloved, believe not every spirit, but try the spirits whether they are of God: because many false prophets are gone out into the world" (1 John 4:1 KJV).

There are many false prophets out there who are parading themselves as powerful ministers of God and are taking advantage of people. They want you to believe them. They want you to accept them as representatives of Jesus's kingdom, and hold them in high esteem. They will do miracles and wonders to show they are powerful, making a show of piousness and displaying their acts of generosity as a manipulative machine to attract following. You must not follow anyone blindly. Understand that false prophets and preachers are not going to present themselves as false, instead they are going to present themselves as genuine. To be able to identify false prophets, you must understand the following truths:

(I).   Signs, miracles, and wonders do not authenticate anyone as genuine man of God. God may not be the source of the miracles, signs and wonders that someone is performing.

> "Many will say to me in that day, Lord, Lord, have we not prophesied in thy name? and in thy name have cast out devils? and in thy name done many wonderful works? [23] And then will I profess unto them, I never knew you: depart from me, ye that work iniquity." (Matthew 7:22-23 KJV).

> "For there shall arise false Christs, and false prophets, and shall shew great signs and wonders; insomuch that, if it were possible, they shall deceive the very elect." (Matthew 24:24 KJV).

(II). Being a philanthropist and giving donations in support of the poor, though it is a good thing to do, does not authenticate anyone as genuine man of God. Openly displayed generosity is designed to be self serving.

"So when you give to the needy, do not announce it with trumpets, as the hypocrites do in the synagogues and on the streets, to be honored by others. Truly I tell you, they have received their reward in full." (Matthew 6:2 NIV).

(III). Being eloquent and versed in the scriptures does not authenticate anyone as genuine man of God.

"For they that are such serve not our Lord Jesus Christ, but their own belly; and by good words and fair speeches deceive the hearts of the simple." (Romans 16:18 KJV).

(IV). Being famous and attracting large following does not authenticate anyone as genuine man of God.

"And many false prophets shall rise, and shall deceive many." (Matthew 24:11 KJV).

Here are few things to beware of, among others, in identifying false prophets:

I.   Beware of anyone whose lifestyle does not reflect the fear of God.

And then will I profess unto them, I never knew you: depart from me, ye that work iniquity." (Matthew 7:23 KJV).

"Nevertheless the foundation of God standeth sure, having this seal, The Lord knoweth them that are his. And, Let every one that nameth the name of Christ depart from iniquity." (2 Timothy 2:19 KJV).

II.   Beware of anyone whose lifestyle is contradictory to the teachings of Christ.

> "Be ye followers of me, even as I also am of Christ."
> (1 Corinthians 11:1 KJV)

III.   Beware of anyone who does evil and wickedness, or prays for evil things to happen to others.

> "You have loved righteousness and hated lawlessness; Therefore God, Your God, has anointed You With the oil of gladness more than Your companions." (Hebrews 1:9 NKJV).

> "But you, O man of God, flee these things and pursue righteousness, godliness, faith, love, patience, gentleness." (1 Timothy 6:11 NKJV).

IV.   Beware of anyone whose passion is what he can gain or becomes in this world.

> "For many walk, of whom I have told you often, and now tell you even weeping, that they are the enemies of the cross of Christ: [19] Whose end is destruction, whose God is their belly, and whose glory is in their shame, who mind earthly things.)" (Philippians 3:18-19 KJV).

V.   Beware of anyone who uses the gospel for financial gain.

> "And it came to pass, as we went to prayer, a certain damsel possessed with a spirit of divination met us, which brought her masters much gain by soothsaying" (Acts 16:16 KJV).

"And through covetousness shall they with feigned words make merchandise of you: whose judgment now of a long time lingereth not, and their damnation slumbereth not." (2 Peter 2:3 KJV).

VI. Beware of anyone who projects himself and not Christ, drawing attention to himself.

"Howbeit when he, the Spirit of truth, is come, he will guide you into all truth: for he shall not speak of himself; but whatsoever he shall hear, that shall he speak: and he will shew you things to come. [14] He shall glorify me: for he shall receive of mine, and shall shew it unto you." (John 16:13-14 KJV).

VII. Beware of anyone who presents himself as being powerful.

"Now for some time a man named Simon had practiced sorcery in the city and amazed all the people of Samaria. He boasted that he was someone great, [10] and all the people, both high and low, gave him their attention and exclaimed, "This man is rightly called the Great Power of God." [11] They followed him because he had amazed them for a long time with his sorcery." (Acts 8:9-11 NIV).

VIII. Beware of anyone who displays and makes a show of power.

"Now for some time a man named Simon had practiced sorcery in the city and amazed all the people of Samaria. He boasted that he was someone great, [10] and all the people, both high and low, gave him their attention and exclaimed, "This man is rightly called the Great Power of God." [11] They followed him because he had amazed them for a long time with his sorcery." (Acts 8:9-11 NIV).

IX.   Beware of anyone who compares himself with others, and making boast of being more anointed and more powerful than the others.

> "We do not dare to classify or compare ourselves with some who commend themselves. When they measure themselves by themselves and compare themselves with themselves, they are not wise." (2 Corinthians 10:12 NIV).

X.   Beware of anyone who says you will be cursed when you leave them.

> "Bless them which persecute you: bless, and curse not." (Romans 12:14 KJV).

XI.   Beware of anyone who teaches in order to create confusion and division.

> "Now I beseech you, brethren, mark them which cause divisions and offences contrary to the doctrine which ye have learned; and avoid them." (Romans 16:17 KJV).

If you are not aware and do not stay vigilant, you will become their victim, and your relationship with God may be interfered with, as predicted by the Apostle Paul when he warned:

> "The Spirit clearly says that in later times some will abandon the faith and follow deceiving spirits and

things taught by demons. [2] Such teachings come through hypocritical liars, whose consciences have been seared as with a hot iron" (1 Timothy 4:1-2 NIV).

Demons do not only creep into churches, but they also seek to gain control of governments by infiltrating the ranks of power and planting ungodly and wicked people in their ranks. They seek to take control of government at all levels so they can influence the formulations of laws and policies that govern the people; that way, they can get satanic laws and policies into the system, thereby paving the way for Satan's rulership through his antichrist. Satan will be the ruler over a people if he can get his own agents seated in the ranks of power and in control of policy decisions.

Demons seek to control human behaviour, by controlling the minds and the reasoning faculties of people. They can make perversion appear ideal and all kinds of atrocities appear as a normal way of living if they can control the minds of people and influence their way of reasoning. Remember, their goal is to establish the government of Satan here on earth.

As you read through the coming chapters of this book, I hope and pray that you will become more aware of the things that are happening in the world around you. This will enable you to step into your authority in Christ Jesus, exercise dominion over all contrary spirits, and enforce God's will in your domain. It is important to understand that it is not the intention of this writer to make the reader become hyper-conscious of demons, such that they begin to see evil spirits everywhere and in everything. You must not be too conscious of evil spirits to the extent and degree that you lose sight of God's presence. It is important to be more conscious of your safety in Christ Jesus, and the working of His power in you. I hope this book enlightens you on the spiritual activities happening around you, and helps you live in Victory.

GIVING MEN AND WOMEN THE RESOURCES AND TOOLS THEY NEED TO SUCCEED IN LIFE AND FULFIL THE REASON FOR WHICH THEY WERE CREATED.

CHAPTER 1

∽❦∽

DEMONS AND THEIR EVIL VICES

The millions of demons that fell with Satan have been unleashed in the world by Satan, and they are working day and night to distort and destroy our social lifestyle. They have infiltrated every fibre of our society with every kind of atrocity, evil imaginations, and all forms of ungodliness. The demon spirits are working to destroy our family institutions and are the causes of divisions in our homes, separations in marriage and divorce, child rebellion, all forms of juvenile delinquency, and all sexual perversions. They are releasing sicknesses and diseases into our world, and they seek to use them to make human beings weak and sickly so that they do not have the strength and stamina to pursue and fulfil the purpose for which they were created.

The demon spirits seek to attack us mentally so that we will become confused, depressed, unbalanced, or disoriented and not be socially and economically responsible and productive. They seek to attack our finances and economic power so that we will live in poverty and not have the power to meet our needs, fund the spread of the gospel, or have the wherewithal to be a blessing to people who are in need.

The devil has declared a war against humans, especially the saints, and against every good thing that God is seeking to do on earth. Make no mistake about it; a lot of what you see around today, all the ungodly, pervasive human behaviour, the hatred, and the killings, are being orchestrated and manipulated by the kingdom of Satan through the activities of demons. Satan knows what God's purpose is for humanity, and he knows that God has chosen the saints to bring his purposes to pass here on earth, and he is fighting dirty to stop that from happening.

Demon spirits are always seeking to have control. Whoever has control over the scheme of things will always be the one who determines a lot of things. Those who are in control are the gatekeepers; they are the influencers; they hold the trigger, and shape events, and make things go in their direction.

Since demons do not have automatic control over human beings, they go about it in a subtle manner to bring people under their subjugation. They use all kinds of schemes, enticements, fear, and seductions to trap people and make them their tools and victims. The human sense is usually their first access point. The senses are powerful, and demons engage the senses to establish a stronghold in people's minds with the intention of using their senses to bring them under their influence. If Satan can have control over how someone's mind works, he will be able to influence the person's entire life in a great deal. What you see, hear, touch, taste, and smell can be the gateway that Satan can use to open your life up to a demon spirit. It is important to note that demons do not seek to gain control over someone just for the sake of it, their intention is always to cause damage. For instance, if demons are able to bring someone into the bondage of drugs, or alcohol addiction, sexual immorality and perversion, they will eventually use that to damage the person's health, rob him of his job, ruin his financial standing, and may also use that to break and destroy every relationship he is having and enjoys.

There are many great careers that were ruined through addictions and many beautiful families deeply damaged, the impact of which may affect many generations ahead. Addictions are powerful tools of damage in the hands of demons. You have got to fight addiction of any kind, reject it, and never let yourself become its next victim; it is a powerful tool of the devil. Demons use addictions to steal, kill and destroy, and there are many lives that they succeeded in cutting short before their time. The people died not having achieved what they came into this world for, bringing shame, pain and grieves to those who love them.

Satan is all out to destroy God's plan for humanity. You can see his handiwork everywhere you go. Satan is an evil and wicked being. His demons are like him: vengeful, venomous, saboteurs, and destructive creatures. Satan and his demons enjoy seeing people suffer and go through pain. They relish it. Here are some more of the atrocities they commit:

- Making people barren in order to hinder the birth of potential heaven's warriors.
- Causing untimely deaths to curtail destiny-fulfilling success.

- Causing road accidents to maim people and incapacitate them.
- Causing miscarriages to create sorrow and unfulfilled dreams.
- Financial theft, to subject people to poverty and the pain of lack, and to hinder the spread of the gospel.
- Marriage wrecking, to ruin children's lives and prospects, thereby destroying destinies.
- Ruining the physical and mental wellbeing of people to make them unfruitful and unproductive in life.
- Causing natural disasters, making the world a harsh place to live in, and making people see God as uncaring.

The list is inexhaustible; there will not be enough room to list out here all the atrocities Satan and demons are committing on earth and in the lives of people. Just look around you, and you will see the devastation they caused and the impact of their atrocities on people. Satan is an inventor of evil; he is an evil genius, and he will do everything to change God's order, and ruin everything if given the chance. You must understand that Satan does not like you; he desires to ruin you, and he is going to try to attack you. Stay on guard; stay close to God.

CHAPTER 2

⁘

DEMONS AND THEIR MANOEUVRES

The devil operates different devices, and he moves in a carefully planned and organised manner. He only deploys the method he considers most lethal against anyone. However, always keep in mind that whatever method he chooses, the goal is to steal, kill, and destroy (John 10:10). Satan is not an omnipresent being; he is only at one place in time and space. However, he has tens of millions of demons, a third of all angelic beings, who fell with him at his disposal, and they are everywhere on the face of the earth, working for Satan, their lord. Demons are spirit beings; they cannot operate in the physical realm without an earthly being or material thing. Therefore, evil spirits make use of human beings to function physically.

A lot of the atrocities and havocs they inflict on earth are orchestrated from the spirit realm and then they are manifested in the physical realm. Their operation in the physical realm is done through human vessels because they cannot directly operate physically. They cannot directly operate in the physical realm because they do not possess physical bodies. Their physical activity in the physical realm occurs in two ways:

1) through mind and mental control of people, this way they can influence people's way of reasoning.
2) through possession, which is the taking of complete control of people's will, mindset, and power of self-determination.

The mind or mental control of people is the devil's main battleground. Demons like to get into one's head and take a seat at the control point of their thoughts. Satan knows that a man's mindset and thought pattern will dictate his actions. So, he seeks to gain control over people's thoughts and lives so that he can, in turn, have control over how they behave. He seeks to have control over all human behaviour and thereby determine what happens in the world. He can control the world if he can dictate how people think, reason, and perceive the world around them and their responses to it. There are many demon-controlled minds out there in the world; they are like zombies, manipulated by spirits. Do not be surprised if someone will not just reason like you do and will consider things that are outrageous and outright evil as wonderful and noble.

This is why you will sometimes see people who are highly educated do crazy and dumb things. This is why many people, including religious leaders, whom you think should know better, do not see some of the sexual perversions being normalised in our generation as something wrong and contradictory to the ordinance of God. Demon control minds see wrong as right, evil as okay, and indecency as decency; they normalise what is not morally right or religiously acceptable, and they are genuinely convinced that they are in the right. Most of the indecent and pervasive things you see people do are a result of demon mind control. This is why it is futile to fight the people, curse them, or hate them. Know that there are evil spirits behind people's reasoning and behaviour. A good understanding of how evil spirits manoeuvre can help you understand people, why they are reasoning the way they do, and how to thrive in your dealings with them. The following are the methods he uses to manipulate people.

❖ Demonic mind control

A particularly good example of demonic mind control in the Bible is where we see Satan taking temporal control of Peter's mind and influencing him to resist Jesus from going to the cross.

> "Then Peter took him, and began to rebuke him, saying, be it far from thee, Lord: this shall not be unto thee. [23] But he turned, and said unto Peter, get thee behind me, Satan: thou art an offence unto me: for thou savourest not the things that be of God, but those that be of men." (Matthew 16:22-23 KJV).

Everyone that was there with Peter and Jesus when he rebuked Jesus, to stop him from going to the cross, would have thought that it was Peter speaking. However, Jesus saw the demon that was behind Peter, and knew that it had momentarily taken control of Peter's thinking faculty. The mind realm is Satan's main battleground, and he seeks to have control over everyone's thinking pattern. Satan knows that he can wreak havoc in our world by influencing what people think, accept, or believe, and thereby manipulating their behaviour and causing them to do his bidding.

Mindset control will lead to behavioural control. Behavioural control is what shapes our world systems and events. Wicked-filled minds will do wicked things. Unholy, ungodly-filled minds will do things that contradict scripture and dishonour God. Murderous thoughts transform people into killers. Pervasive behaviour, immorality, envy, wickedness, etc. are all due to demonic mind control. If Satan imbeds his ideology in anyone's mind, he can get people to live his way of life. Satan uses pictures; he comes through dreams; he uses ungodly companionships and negative and ungodly conversations to infiltrate and manipulate the mind. This is why a believer must beware of the things he is watching, who he is in intimate relationships with, and who he spends much time with, and the things he is listening to.

Satan cannot influence a believer's behaviour unless he can gain control of his mind. The mind cannot be liberated from demonic control until the word of God enters. The word of God is the only powerful tool that has the capacity to impact people's thinking patterns and transform them. This is why the Bible says in Romans 12:2:

> "And be not conformed to this world: but be ye transformed by the renewing of your mind, that ye may prove what is that good, and acceptable, and perfect, will of God" (KJV).

No one can live a godly life until he experiences the renewing of his mind through the power of the word of God. As someone commits himself to the study of the word and approaches it with simplicity, submitting himself to the work of the Holy Spirit, the Word will gain entrance into his thinking and reasoning faculty and do a powerful work of transformation. And as a result, his way of reasoning will change, and he will start to see everything as God sees it. This is possible because the word of God transforms the human mind and brings it into sync with God's mind. It is not possible to have the mind of God, to see things as He sees them, until the word of God gains entry into the mind and transforms it:

> "The entrance and unfolding of Your words give light; their unfolding gives understanding (discernment and comprehension) to the simple" (Psalm 119:130 AMPC).

There are no vacuums in the spirit realm. It is either one's mind, through the transformational power of God's word, is in sync with God's reasoning, or through the deprivation of the word, demons gain access and exert their control of the mind. A demon-controlled mind is doomed, it is the most lethal weapon on earth. It can devise and manufacture all kinds of evil and destructive weapons, and this is why Satan covets rulership of the human mind and thinking pattern. God flooded and destroyed the people of Noah's generation because the Bible says, God looked and saw that the thoughts of their hearts were geared towards perpetuating evil on earth.

> "The Lord saw that the wickedness of man was great in the earth, and that every imagination and intention of all human thinking was only evil

continually. [6] And the Lord regretted that He had made man on the earth, and He was grieved at heart" (Genesis 6:5-6 AMPC).

No man can truly live the God-like kind of life without a transformed mind. Until people start to see things differently and see the world around them differently, and in the light of God's word, they cannot prove what is good, acceptable, and the perfect will of God. God says:

> "For my thoughts are not your thoughts, neither are your ways my ways," declares the LORD. [9] "As the heavens are higher than the earth, so are my ways higher than your ways and my thoughts than your thoughts" (Isaiah 55:8-9 NIV).

In this scripture, God makes it clear that no one's way of life can be God's way, except God's thoughts become his thoughts. To expect someone who has not experienced the renewing of the mind, through the transforming power of the word of God, to live the Christian life is like asking a camel to go through the eye of a needle. Mind control is referred to as demonic obsession, and it is different from demonic possession.

❖ Demonic oppression

Demonic oppression occurs when demons keep someone under subjection and hardship, depriving them of their peaceful life and the freedom to enjoy living. In demonic oppression, evil spirits exert authority over the person, and are doing horrible things to the person, hindering him from achieving happiness or fulfilment.

Demonic oppression may come in different shapes or forms. It may take the form of demon possession. However, in demon oppression, the demon is not only possessing someone to use him to serve their purpose physically. When it involves oppression, the demon possessing someone will subject the person to horrific punishments and painful life experiences. A case study here is the story about a boy in the gospel of Mark whose demons would periodically get him to throw himself in the fire.

> "A man in the crowd answered, "Teacher, I brought you my son, who is possessed by a spirit that has robbed him of speech. [18] Whenever it seizes him, it throws him to the ground. He foams at the mouth, gnashes his teeth, and becomes rigid. I asked your disciples to drive out the spirit, but they could not." [19] "You unbelieving generation," Jesus replied, "how long shall I stay with you? How long shall I put up with you? Bring the boy to me." [20] So they brought him. When the spirit saw Jesus, it immediately threw the boy into a convulsion. He fell to the ground and rolled around, foaming at the mouth. [21] Jesus asked the boy's father, "How long has he been like this?" "From childhood," he answered. [22] "It has often thrown him into fire or water to kill him. But if you can do anything, take pity on us and help us." (Mark 9:17-22 NIV)

The demons that possessed this boy were very wicked demons of oppression. They would oftentimes have him convulse and throw himself into the fire or water to kill him. You can imagine the pain he would experience, the number of times he almost got drowned, and the burns he would have had all over his body, as he got thrown into the fire. That is an example of the oppression of demons. Another example of oppression is when someone is gripped by fear so much that they cannot take the initiative to do what they need to do. They are under the power of fear, such that they cannot move. Another example of demonic oppression is the grip of anxiety on someone. Some people are constantly unsettled; they are anxious and worrying unnecessarily, even when they are not able to put their finger on anything tangible that is a reason to worry about. They suffer from anxiety so much that they are unable to function effectively. Some people experience anxiety whenever they are in a crowd, and they do not go to large gatherings. Some have anxiety about flying, so they cannot travel abroad. Anxiety causes them sleepless nights and makes them sick, and it limits them. These are the oppressions of the devil.

Satan is using demonic oppression to steal their peace, their joy in life, their joy in relationships, and to hold someone back from maximising their potential. Having constant nightmares can also be an oppression of the devil. Consistent miscarriages may be an oppression of the devil. A constant loss of investment may be an oppression of the devil. The constant end of marriage engagement may be an oppression of the devil. Unnecessary delays may be an oppression of the devil. Simply put, oppression is Satan's manoeuvre to steal joy, and subject someone to a perpetual life of struggles, misery, and pain.

Unforgiveness, bitterness, nurturing of hurts, and even envy are avenues that demons use to have access to people to oppress them. Demons use unforgiveness and bitterness to cause depression and related illnesses. Depression is lethal, and there are demons behind it. They take advantage of someone's misfortune and vulnerability to latch on to him. They use someone's challenges, which they have created, to make him feel less of himself, not fit, useless, a failure, etc. These demons make the oppressed believe that he or she is in the situation because they are no good people, that God is against them, that the world is against them, that no one cares, and that life is not worth living.

Your life is worth living, irrespective of what you are experiencing right now. God has a fantastic plan for your future, and Satan is using your challenge to hinder it, but I assure you, there is help for you out there. Please speak to someone if you are having suicidal thoughts. There is someone at the other end of the phone who would be happy to assist you, if only you could pick up the courage and ring them. Reach out to one of the numbers below today if you are in the UK and speak to someone.

Samaritans – for everyone Call 116 123 Email jo@samaritans.org
Information:
Campaign Against Living Miserably (CALM) Call 0800585858 – 5pm to midnight everyday. Visit the webchat page
Information:
Papyrus – prevention of young suicide HOPELINE247 Call 08000684141 Text 07860039967. Email pat@papyrus-uk.org
Information:
Childline – for children and young people under 19 Call 08001111 – the number will not show up on your phone bill.

Information:

SOS Silence of Suicide – for everyone Call 03001020505 – 4pm
    to midnight everyday. Email support@sossilenceofsuicide.
    org

Message a text line

If you do not want to talk to someone over the phone, these
text lines are open 24 hours a day, everyday.

Information:

Shout Crisis Text Line – for everyone

Text "SHOUT" to 85258

Information:

Young Minds Crisis Messenger – for people under 19

Text "YM" to 85258

(https://www.nhs.uk/mental-health/feelings-symptoms-
behaviours/behaviours/help-for-suicidal-thoughts/).

Misfortune, disappointments, setbacks, and failure are normal
occurrences in life; they do not happen to anyone because they
are bad people; they happen because these evil spirits orchestrate
them and use them to further wreak havoc on people and to
kill. A lot of the people who experience crises are exceptionally
gifted and have a great destiny. Satan may not know all about
your future, but he can smell a special person from a distance.
He will not bother about you if there is no greatness inside of
you. No matter what, do not let the devil steal your joy; do not
let him cut you off from loved ones; reject suicidal thoughts;
there is more to your life than you think. Satan is only using
the troubles he created for you to blur your vision from seeing
what is ahead of you and what you can achieve.

Social violence is another evil vice that comes from the spirit of
oppression. Social violence does not take root and express itself

in one day; it stems from unforgiveness, fear, an inferiority complex, and a lack of contentment. Most people who are under the control of this demon and they abuse people, were victims of social injustice or abuse at some point in their lives. Do not allow the devil to hold you captive to social violence; do not engage in social violence, do not accept it; do not tolerate it. Speak to someone and report it to the larger family. If you stay captive to social violence, it can make you unproductive, antisocial, depressed, steal your joy of living, or even kill you. On the other hand, you, as a victim, may be turned into a monster by it. There are mothers who maltreat their children because they are in abusive relationships. There are kids who did terrible things to other kids because they were victims of social violence themselves. The person who is being abused today may end up doing harm to the abuser and get into trouble with the law.

There are other gateways these demons make use of to access people to oppress them, which you need to avoid. To keep clear of these demons, stay clear of anything satanic; stay clear of tarot cards, palm reading, and all forms of sexual perversion and immorality. And do not keep feeding your mind with horror and violent-related things. If you are a parent, you should monitor the stuff your children watch on TV. Do not allow your kids to have access to materials that are meant for adults because they help to shape their minds. Do not harbour hurt or unforgiveness. Stay clear of bitterness because it is a gateway. Bitterness is one of the quickest ways demons gain access to people's minds and control them. If you start to see yourself drifting and starting to entertain such, you must go to God quickly and ask Him to restore and heal you of every hurt and pain. You may also need to seek counsel and prayer from your man of God. God equips and anoints every person He calls into the pastoral ministry; your pastor is anointed and can stand with you to cast out every spirit.

❖ Demonic attacks and afflictions

A demonic attack is Satan's attempt to disrupt or destroy something about someone to cause him pain and make him lose confidence in God's word. Demonic attacks come in various forms. It could be an attack against a pregnancy and causing miscarriages; it could come in the form of causing road accidents, it could be an attack against your business; it could be an arrow of sickness or disease. Some of these incurable diseases are caused by demons. There is a story of a woman in the Bible who Satan had kept under affliction, and was crippled by a spirit for eighteen years, and who Jesus delivered.

> "And a woman was there who had been crippled by a spirit for eighteen years. She was bent over and could not straighten up at all. [12] When Jesus saw her, he called her forward and said to her, "Woman, you are set free from your infirmity." [13] Then he put his hands on her, and immediately she straightened up and praised God" (Luke 13:11-13 NIV)

Demons like to attack whatever is important to someone and ruin it, the essence of which is to afflict and cause pain. Demonic attacks become an affliction when someone keeps experiencing the same attack over a lengthy period, or the problem caused as a result of the attack is sustained over a lengthy period. For instance, it becomes an affliction when someone who was fired from his job keeps getting fired, wherever he works or fails to secure new employment over a long period of time. It becomes an affliction if miscarriages keep occurring and the pregnancy never reaches term. Demons will not only attack to cause pain, but they will also seek to perpetuate people's pain, so that their victims will languish and live in misery until they are destroyed, or they renounce Jesus as their Lord.

❖ Demonic possession

Demonic possession happens when a demon or demons take possession of the human body and the mind of someone, and they bring the person's spirit into subjugation. In demonic possession, there will be an indwelling of evil spirits inside the possessed. Possession is different from demonic mind control or oppression. Fundamentally, where demonic possession occurs, a demon spirit or spirits would have complete control over someone and become the main driver in the person's life. In other words, because the possessed person is housing demons, the demons who have made their home inside the person will have control over his mind, his spirit, and his body, and can determine the outcome of his life and experience here on earth until he is set free. The case of the mad man Jesus encountered at the shore of Gerasenes is a typical example of demonic possession.

> "When Jesus got out of the boat, a man with an
> impure spirit came from the tombs to meet him.
> [3] This man lived in the tombs, and no one could
> bind him anymore, not even with a chain. [4] For
> he had often been chained hand and foot, but he
> tore the chains apart and broke the irons on his

feet. No one was strong enough to subdue him. [5] Night and day among the tombs and in the hills he would cry out and cut himself with stones. [6] When he saw Jesus from a distance, he ran and fell on his knees in front of him. [7] He shouted at the top of his voice, "What do you want with me, Jesus, Son of the Most High God? In God's name do not torture me!" [8] For Jesus had said to him, "Come out of this man, you impure spirit!" [9] Then Jesus asked him, "What is your name?" "My name is Legion," he replied, "for we are many." [10] And he begged Jesus again and again not to send them out of the area. [11] A large herd of pigs was feeding on the nearby hillside. [12] The demons begged Jesus, "Send us among the pigs; allow us to go into them." [13] He gave them permission, and the impure spirits came out and went into the pigs. The herd, about two thousand in number, rushed down the steep bank into the lake and were drowned." (Mark 5:2-13 NIV).

Note that it is not in every case of demon possession that the possessed becomes mad or subjugated to physical affliction, such that it is obvious for all to see, as in the case of the man in the passage above. Some demon possessions are accompanied by oppressions and afflictions, but in some possessions, demons simply come inside someone's body to control and manipulate him for their purpose, and the possessed person may go about his life, appearing as normal as everyone else. One of such cases of demon possessions is the possession of Judas Iscariot.

"And the chief priests and scribes sought how they might kill him; for they feared the people. [3] Then entered Satan into Judas surnamed Iscariot, being of the number of the twelve. [4] And he went his way, and communed with the chief priests and captains, how he might betray him unto them." (Luke 22:2-4 KJV).

When Satan entered Judas' body, Judas did not convulse; he did not go about naked; he did not leave home to sleep in the tombs; he simply became a house for demons, and they used him to serve their purpose. There are many people out there housing demons, but they physically appear normal and sound-minded, however, they are being used by the demons who have occupied their bodies to achieve Satan's agenda here on earth.

Now, it is important to understand that a believer in Christ cannot experience demon possession. In the sense that he becomes a home for evil spirits, and they have the control over his mind, body, subjugate his spirit, and manipulate his life and wellbeing. It is not possible for a believer whose body has become the house of the Holy Spirit to at the same time be a house for demons. There is no such fellowship between light and darkness:

> "Don't you know that you yourselves are God's temple and that God's Spirit dwells in your midst?" (1 Corinthians 3:16 NIV).

> "What agreement is there between the temple of God and idols? For we are the temple of the living God. As God has said: "I will live with them and walk among them, and I will be their God, and they will be my people." (2 Corinthians 6:16 NIV).

There is a significant difference between the lives of Old Testament saints and the lives of New Testament believers. The fundamental difference is the fact that, in the Old Testament era, no one was born again, no one had become the temple of God, and no one had the Holy Spirit dwelling inside of him. Someone would say, *but what about Judas?* He was a disciple of Jesus, and yet a demon possessed him. Realise that Judas lived in the Old Testament era. It was Jesus who fulfilled the Old Testament dispensation by his death on the cross and ushered in the New Testament when he resurrected from the dead, having purchased redemption for all. Human beings could not become God's temple before the death and resurrection of Jesus. The Holy Spirit began living inside human beings only after the redemption of the human soul. Before then, the Holy Spirit only comes upon someone temporarily, to empower him for an assignment, and after the assignment is completed, the Holy Spirit will lift. He could not live on the inside of anyone because no one had experienced redemption. The Old Testament saints could prophesy, perform miracles, and do extraordinary things only when the Spirit of God came upon them, but glory be to God, today the Holy Spirit resides inside of us who believe and have accepted Jesus as Lord and Saviour.

The temple of God, which is in the heart of the born-again believer, cannot be co-occupied by the Holy Spirit and an evil spirit simultaneously. All the cases of demon possessions recorded in the New Testament occurred to the people who operated in the Old Testament. All the people of Jesus's era were all Old Testament saints until His death and resurrection. Demon possession does not take place in a believer because the inside of him has already become the house of the Holy Spirit, and a demon spirit cannot have the same dwelling with the Spirit of God; there cannot be a fellowship between them in any form. Therefore, the teachings that support the idea that a believer can be possessed by an evil spirit contradict the scriptures. To have a good understanding of this aspect, it is critical to know what demon possession really is. Believers often experience attacks, oppression, affliction, or manipulation. Satan and his Demons are liars; lying is their language, and they thrive through lies.

> "For you are the children of your father the devil, and you love to do the evil things he does. He was a murderer from the beginning. He has always hated the truth because there is no truth in him. When he lies, it is consistent with his character; for he is a liar and the father of lies" (John 8:44 NLT).

Satan wants believers to believe the lie that he has the power to come on inside of them, possess them, and rule in their lives and affairs, but it is only a lie; he has no such power. The knowledge of the truth sets people free from Satan's lies, influence, and control. The truth is that believers have received deliverance from the power of darkness, the very day Jesus became their Saviour and Lord. The Bible says:

> "Giving thanks unto the Father, which hath made us meet to be partakers of the inheritance of the saints in light: [13] Who hath delivered us from the power of darkness, and hath translated us into the kingdom of his dear Son" (Colossians 1:12-13 KJV).

The believer no longer belongs to the kingdom of darkness. Satan lost his right to him completely the day the Holy Spirit came on the inside of him. If you are a believer, you have got to know this. Because you no longer belong to the kingdom of Satan, he has no right to your spirit, soul, and body and cannot determine the outcome of your life or your wellbeing here on earth. It is therefore important that you do not entertain the fear of becoming demon possessed. You have the power to cast out demons, never entertain the lies of the devil that you can't, and never nurse the fear that you may be possessed by a demon when you try to cast them out; you will not. The Bible says:

> "You, dear children, are from God and have overcome them, because the one who is in you is greater than the one who is in the world." (1 John 4:4 NIV).

CHAPTER 3

◦——— ⟨⬦⟩ ———◦

STRUCTURE AND OPERATIONAL SYSTEM OF SATAN'S KINGDOM

The Bible in Ephesians 6:12 shows us four levels of Satan's hierarchical structure in which his kingdom is organised, and how his operational systems are driven.

"For we wrestle not against flesh and blood, but against principalities, against powers, against the rulers of the darkness of this world, against spiritual wickedness in high places." (Ephesians 6:12 KJV).

The four hierarchical structures identified in the scripture above are:

- the principalities
- the powers
- the rulers of darkness in this world
- the spiritual wickedness in high places.

Satan has structured his demons into an operational system to achieve his evil purposes. Each level has a responsibility for a specific assignment. Paul the apostle, in 2 Corinthians 10:4-5, gives us an insight into the operations of these demon spirits according to their hierarchical structure. It is important to be well informed about their operations and not be ignorant, because it is at each of these levels of their operations that our arsenal against the kingdom of darkness must be directed for us to dislodge and incapacitate them. Let us consider 2 Corinthians 10:4-5 for a deeper understanding.

> "For though we walk in the flesh, we do not war after the flesh: [4] (For the weapons of our warfare are not carnal, but mighty through God to the pulling down of strong holds; [5] Casting down imaginations, and every high thing that exalteth itself against the knowledge of God, and bringing into captivity every thought to the obedience of Christ; [6] And having in a readiness to revenge all disobedience, when your obedience is fulfilled." (2 Corinthians 10:3-6 KJV).

Drawing from the scripture above, it is clear that believers have been given immensely powerful weapons capable of bringing every demon under subjection, regardless of their hierarchy. Anytime a believer deploys the weapons of our warfare, it is accompanied by the might of God, and demons cannot overcome it. There are four hierarchical structures of demon spirits' operations, and they function to achieve four fundamental things:

- To establish strongholds.
- To plant perverse and wicked imaginations.
- To raise high things that would exalt themselves against the knowledge of God.

- To instil disobedient thoughts.

To understand which hierarchy of demons is responsible for each of the outcomes above, you will have to look at 2 Corinthians 10:3-6 together with Ephesians 6:12. The two scriptural references bring to light the operations of the kingdom of darkness.

❖ Principalities - the Strongholds spirits

Another name for the principalities is Authority. The principalities are the spirits who are responsible for establishing strongholds or authority in a place, for the kingdom of Satan, and they hold the ground there. The satanic strongholds are formed when the kingdom of darkness succeeds in establishing a base or presence, has taken complete control, and has a principality overseeing the domain. The domain can be a family, town, city, any establishment, schools, even a church, over someone. The devil's stronghold is that place where he has completely taken over and is fully installed as authority, and he is fully in charge. Satanic strongholds do not come about in one day; they happen through a process of time and through the activities of the other demonic hierarchies that work to bring them about.

Typically, a principality is the last to arrive in a place. A principality only comes into a place after the coast has been cleared and the ground is prepared. This is why there is nothing insignificant or done just for the sake of it when a demon is influencing someone. The reality is, once someone yields to a demon spirit and the demon spirit establishes some level of control, the demon will create an opening for other demons of his kind to come in, and as they get the person to form a habit of doing what they are inside him to do, he gets trapped, and before he realises it, they will bring in a demon who is an authority or a principality to establish a stronghold. A demon in the hierarchy of authority or principality only comes into a place to make it a stronghold. Establishing a satanic stronghold brings the victim or place under the complete rulership of the kingdom of darkness.

Satanic strongholds can be passed from one generation to another. For instance, the devil can form a stronghold in a family by establishing a habit of drunkenness, by putting in a family the root of suicide, a heritage of mental illness, or the yoke of divorce. These are then passed from one generation to the next. There would be a stronghold spirit in operation when a particular destructive behaviour, misfortune, a type of death, poverty, a type of sickness, or disease appeared to follow in a family line and through generations. The devil is a legalist, he likes to claim rights or hold the ground. When he is allowed in a place, over time he establishes a stronghold in the place.

One of the ways Satan establishes a stronghold is through a covenant. Any form of covenant with the devil, by someone who is a head over a family, can give the devil charge over an entire generation. A covenant with the devil by the head of a family can, for instance, establish a satanic altar in that family and may invite a stronghold spirit into the family, and he will exist in the family as a god for a long time. I have mentioned earlier that stronghold spirits are demons who operate at the level of principality, and they come to stay and hold garrison for Satan in a place over a prolonged period. They are gatekeepers.

And because they are gatekeepers, you are only able to clear their domain from all demons when you deinstall them. Their presence in a place gives all the other demons a free pass to operate there.

❖ Powers—the spirits behind imagination

The demons that are at the power level are spirits who are responsible for reshaping, redesigning, and reorganising the world system to make it satanic in all ramifications. They are experts at manipulating people's thoughts and imaginations. The power demon spirits are solely responsible for evil imaginations, ungodly thoughts, and perversions in the world. The thoughts and imaginations of man are very powerful. Demons that operate within the cadre of powers become very powerful and do great havoc on earth when they gain control over the thoughts and imaginations of people. So, they work to take hold of one's thoughts, and to pervert his way of thinking and reasoning, thereby influencing the way one views himself, views people, and views the world around him. Powers exert control and influence in the world by reinforcing Satan's ideology and ways.

The spirits that are in the realm of power are also lying spirits; their main task is to pollute the mind, and plant in the mind the things Satan wants people to believe. It is these demons that make a serial killer, a rapist, a paedophile, and all the other twisted-minded people out there. They cause people to be distorted in their thinking so that morality and decency do not make sense to them, such that they are able to do the unthinkable without feeling guilty or having any remorse.

The spirits behind imaginations make use of all sorts of tools to capture human thoughts and influence them. They employ such things as pornography, horror movies, promos on billboards, books, and magazines. This is why people need to beware of the things they listen to, behold, or watch, and to never allow themselves to get hooked on anything. You must understand that a lot of what you see displayed in the physical world has a satanic agenda, is not random; it may appear as nothing, but demons exploit it to create gateways.

The power demons also operate through dreams and false prophecy. Everything they inspire is geared toward influencing your imagination. For instance, they can make you see your mother or your spouse hurting you in a dream. They can speak to you in a lying prophecy and present someone close to you as the reason for your downfall, and if you don't have discernment, you are going to start a war with the people that care for you the most, the people God positioned in your life to help propel you to your destiny.

Today, the human mind is experiencing an attack that no generation has witnessed before. My heart goes out to the young people of this generation; they are being bombarded, left, right, and center, in a way we did not experience in the past. What was once abominable in many societies and considered unacceptable to human culture is now being freely highlighted on our streets, aired on television stations, and occupying the front covers of magazines and newspapers. The invention of the internet and digital world contributed to making things even more challenging, so much so that parents today must work harder than ever before to track their children and help protect them from predators that roam viciously in cyberspace.

Today, young people like to look skinny and dress up looking sexy because the world has painted a picture in their imaginations of what the 'ideal image' should be. And most of what is perceived as the ideal is completely indecent and inappropriate. The devil is doing an overtime in the realm of the imagination because he knows the Bible said, a man is what he imagines in his heart, (Proverbs 23:7). An indication that the power spirits have been terribly busy and have recorded a significant amount of success is the prevalent behavioural decadence we see in our world today. Human beings' imaginations are being invaded from all angles by evil spirits and as a result we are witnessing increasing atrocities, wickedness, and unimaginable destruction all around the world.

❖ The rulers of darkness in this world—the spirits that raise high things that exalt themselves against the knowledge of God—

The devil is doing everything he can to erase God from our society, and he is using methods and mechanisms that appear to be harmless and modern ideas. Though there are more profound practices such as witchcraft, Satanism, and all the other forms of occult groups, which are the by-product of the work of the influence of the rulers of darkness, however, he also uses a more subtle, and harmless means to try to erase the knowledge of God. Getting the knowledge of God erased in the world is Satan's most lethal weapon. The devil knows that if he can erase God from the world system, he will be able to take away the fear of God in the world. The effort to erase the knowledge of God in a society is Satan's oldest tactics, which he deploys against every generation. Wherever he is able to achieve success, he also succeeds in instilling evil as a replacement. We can see the example of this in the history of Israel in their walk with God.

> "And also all that generation were gathered unto their fathers: and there arose another generation after them, which knew not the LORD, nor yet the works which he had done for Israel. [11] And the children of Israel did evil in the sight of the LORD, and served Baalim: [12] And they forsook the LORD God of their fathers, which brought them out of the land of Egypt, and followed other gods, of the gods of the people that were round about them, and bowed themselves unto them, and provoked the LORD to anger." (Judges 2:10-12 KJV).

It is the knowledge of God that instils the fear of God in people, and the fear of GOD will be absent where there is no knowledge of God. Furthermore, the fear of God motivates a person to adhere to and subject themselves to certain moral and godly values. Without the knowledge and fear of God, people will live their lives as it pleases them and would have no restraint, and as a result, all kinds of vices and atrocities will permeate society. The fundamental task of the rulers of the darkness of this world is to introduce another way of life to our society, which is devoid of God. When someone does not believe in God, he does not accept the concept of creation, he does not feel accountable to God, he does not accept that there is life after death, he thinks death is the end of life, and that is the place Satan seeks to bring everyone to. Satan is only able to position himself as a god if he can create a world where the Almighty God does not exist. Apart from trying to erase the knowledge of God from the world, rulers of darkness seek rulership on behalf of Satan.

Ruler spirits are sub-rulers; in other words, they operate to establish control and enforce the will of a principality. Ruler spirits seek to rule in every segment of society, e.g., a community, a neighbourhood, schools, companies, and government institutions. Since they are spirits and cannot operate in the physical realm, they orchestrate a way for their human vessels or agents to be in positions of power and influence so they can control policies and decision-making and flood the world system with policies that promote Satan's agenda.

Ruler spirits target people in the echelon of power so they can control the world system. Their human vessels are usually the high and mighty, and the shakers are the movers of society, and they are deeply entrenched in Satanism, the underworld, witchcraft, and all the other powerful cult groups that are operating in the dark corners and hidden from the ordinary man. Corrupt governments, evil dictatorships, a strong satanic presence in a community, and even the various cartels are their signatures in a place.

The rulers of the darkness of this world are also wicked spirits. They create troubling situations, devastations, and wastes to defy the Word of God. They create scenes to make people doubt the existence of God, doubt the love or power of God, or even believe in God. They like to make the Word of God appear powerless and outdated.

❖ Disobedient spirits—the spiritual wickedness in high places

Disobedient spirits are at the fourth level of the operational system of the kingdom of darkness. They may appear at the bottom of the satanic hierarchy, but they are demons that create havoc and great devastation. Disobedient spirits are the foot soldiers, and on a day-to-day, minute-to-second they carry out the devil's grand vision of stealing, killing, and destroying. These demons' sole responsibility is to create disobedience or rebellion, first against the authority of God and then against any godly system in place. These spirits enjoy afflicting the poor and the weak. They are behind every form of rebellion, juvenile-related offenses, drug addiction, gun and knife crime, burglary, murder, and all forms of antisocial behaviour.

Spiritual wickedness in high places is behind child abuse, woman abuse, and all the evil you see in your streets. They are everywhere and littered like leeches. They influence fathers to walk away from their families; they influence marriage to divorce, so children will be without role models. They create rapists, drug dealers, and serial killers to cause pain. They are responsible for the violence, confusion, greed, hate, murder, suicide, rebellion, fear, lust, pervasion, and all the evil and immoral activities that we see all around us or hear about. These spirits want to influence our lifestyle to make us lose our humanity and become enemies to one another. They seek to afflict us with diseases and cause all kinds of accidents. These demon spirits are behind wars, murders, genocides, and all the killings. They seek to disrupt the plan of God for humanity, and their assignment is to make Satan a god.

The four demons' hierarchies are in perfect sync, and they collaborate intelligently, networking to build Satan's kingdom. No aspect of each of the hierarchy's assignment is detached from the operation of the other and stands in isolation. They rely on what each is doing to install a principality in a place, and pave way for the coming, and the reign of the Antichrist. Never take for granted, or deal lightly, with whatever you realise that demons are behind them. Things may look ordinary but in the grand scheme of things nothing is. Everything in the physical is controlled in the realm of the spirit. There are no vacuums at all. To stop evil we must engage in warfare with evil spirits and defeat them. Jesus gave us power to trample upon them. You must learn to fight the good fight of faith (1 Timothy 6:12). Fight to maintain your liberty in Christ Jesus (Galatians 5:1). Fight to push back evil and wicked spirits from your domain. Fight for your inheritance.

CHAPTER 4

—•——⌒◆⌒——•—

DEMONS IN HUMAN BEINGS

> "Look, I have given you authority over all the power of the enemy, and you can walk among snakes and scorpions and crush them. Nothing will injure you" (Luke 10:19 NLT).

D emons are spirit beings; they do not have physical bodies and can therefore not operate in the physical realm without the use of human agents. A substantial portion of the atrocities that demons create here on earth are through the human beings that they possess or influence. You are going to encounter human beings who are under the influence of demons wherever you go; you cannot avoid them while you are on earth, and they will try to interfere with your life. Do not be concerned about that if you have a relationship with Jesus, for in Christ Jesus, you have authority over snakes and scorpions and over all the power of the enemy. You must never be afraid of what evil people can do to you.

> "In God have I put my trust and confident reliance;
> I will not be afraid. What can man do to me"
> (Psalm 56:11 AMPC).

Though evil is present everywhere, believers in Christ also have enormous power and authority vested in them to walk among them victoriously. Jesus said, *nothing will injure you.* You must go about your life in the strength of Jesus's word.

The snakes and the scorpions are not literal, they are metaphors; they represent demon spirits in their kinds, or the venoms that the human agents they possess, and influence to do their bidding, are carrying. There are people who operate as snakes, scorpions, or wolves wherever you go, they are positioned there by Satan. For instance, Jesus called the Pharisees vipers in Matthew 3:7. He called them serpents and vipers in Matthew 23:33. Jesus also called Herod fox in Luke 13:32. He referred our mixing and dealings with the rest of the world as being among wolves (Luke 10:3). These are all metaphors, describing the types of spirits that operate in people who have not met Jesus, whose lives have not been transformed by Him. I like to give a further insight into what they represent for your easy identification of them.

❖ The snakes and vipers

Snakes are venomous reptiles; they come in varied species and are dangerous. Snakes kill easily by releasing their venom into someone's bloodstream when they bite them. Snakes release their venom simply to kill, not just to hurt. Snakes in this context represent the types of people who kill; they attack you in the dark, they attack you when you are not observant, they come into your life as friends, but they are only seeking an opportunity to poison you or poison what you have. They will release their poison to kill what is important to you without a thought, and they will not have a sleepless night about it. They will kill your relationship if they can; they will kill your career, business, etc.

Another word for snakes is serpent. The serpent represents death, evil, and destruction. The serpent is the form that Satan took in his fallen state, and the Bible calls him the ancient serpent.

> "The great dragon was hurled down that ancient serpent called the devil, or Satan, who leads the whole world astray. He was hurled to the earth, and his angels with him" (Revelation 12:9 NIV).

This explains why Satan's primary focus is to steal, kill, and to destroy (John 10:10). The people who can be referred to as serpents, are the people who are treacherous, who exploit privileged positions of trust, as Lucifer did (before he became Satan and the devil), and cause havoc. You do not toy with snakes, because no matter how familiar you get with them, they can be dangerously aggressive, and unpredictable. Hate is a snake poison. John the Apostle says that anyone who hates his brother is a murderer.

> "Anyone who hates a brother or sister is a murderer, and you know that no murderer has eternal life residing in him" (1 John 3:15 NIV).

Anyone who is harbouring hatred is operating with the snake spirit; he can evilly kill someone. You must be careful with the people who hate you. Be careful with the space you grant them in your life; they will kill you easily or kill what is dear to you before you realise it. Jesus called those who killed, who have crucified and persecuted the prophets and teachers of the Word of God, a generation of vipers.

> "Ye serpents, ye generation of vipers, how can ye escape the damnation of hell? [34] Wherefore, behold, I send unto you prophets, and wise men, and scribes: and some of them ye shall kill and crucify; and some of them shall ye scourge in your synagogues, and persecute them from city to city" (Matthew 23:33-34 KJV).

A viper who bit Paul when they shipwrecked and landed on the island of Melita did not only want to kill him but also wanted to discredit his ministry and the message of the gospel of Jesus, which he bore. It sought to kill Paul to present him as a murderer and to make the gospel have no effect.

> "And when Paul had gathered a bundle of sticks, and laid them on the fire, there came a viper out of the heat, and fastened on his hand. [4] And when the barbarians saw the venomous beast hang on his hand, they said among themselves, no doubt this man is a murderer, whom, though he hath escaped the sea, yet vengeance suffereth not to live" (Acts 28:3-4 KJV).

The viper latched itself on Paul's hand to lie to the people that he was an evil man and to discredit his message of the gospel, but glory be to God, Paul shook it into the fire, demonstrating the believers' power and authority over snakes and scorpions. There are many people you will encounter who carry the snakes and the vipers' spirits; they will seek to destroy whatever you have by making your efforts fail, but Jesus says you have the power to walk among them and nothing will injure you. Don't fear them or fear what they are planning, but don't be oblivious to their presence either.

❖ The scorpions

When Rehoboam, the king of Israel, told the representative of the people, who came to ask for succour from the weight his father Solomon put on them, but instead he told them that he was going to chastise them with scorpions, they understood exactly what he meant; he was going to cause them more pain.

> "And now whereas my father did lead you with a heavy yoke, I will add to your yoke: my father hath chastised you with whips, but I will chastise you with scorpions" (1 Kings 12:11 KJV).

Scorpions are the people Satan deploys and positions to cause people pain. They will sting to cause pain whenever they get the chance. Scorpions will always look out for what they know can hurt someone if they touch it, and they will touch it to hurt them. You must be aware of the people around you who often do things to hurt you, to make you go through harsh and uncomfortable situations. Be vigilant of individuals who derive pleasure from causing you harm or revel in your suffering. Be observant and notice which people seem happy when you are hurting; they are the scorpions.

> "And they had tails like unto scorpions, and there were stings in their tails: and their power was to hurt men for five months" (Revelation 9:10 KJV).

You can identify scorpions by how they relate to you; they are scorpions if they are always stinging you, causing you pain, making you cry, causing you losses, and getting you into trouble. They are scorpions, even if they are always coming back and saying sorry for it. Scorpions may cause you some hurt, but they cannot injure your destiny; they have no power to incapacitate you completely. You have authority over all the powers of the enemy.

❖ The foxes

Foxes are spoilers, they come to ruin the fruits of your labour. They will do anything to mess you up, spoil your work, and close the door to your success. Foxes do not want you to enjoy the fruits of your labour or investments so they will steal it or ruin it. For instance, if you keep a farm, a poultry farm especially, you do not want to have a fox in the vicinity, it will feed on your farm and rob you of the profit.

> "Take us the foxes, the little foxes, that spoil the vines: for our vines have tender grapes" (Song of Songs 2:15 KJV)

Samson's use of foxes to ruin the harvests from the farm of the Philistines was not a coincidence; he understood the destructive nature of foxes—they are spoilers by nature.

> "Samson said, "This time I cannot be blamed for everything I am going to do to you Philistines." [4] Then he went out and caught 300 foxes. He tied their tails together in pairs, and he fastened a torch to each pair of tails. [5] Then he lit the torches

and let the foxes run through the grain fields of
the Philistines. He burned all their grain to the
ground, including the sheaves and the uncut grain.
He also destroyed their vineyards and olive groves"
(Judges 15:3-5 NLT).

Foxes are the people that come around you, or the people you
engage with, who just want to ruin your efforts and subject you
to losses. They are the people who sneak behind you to take
what belongs to you when you are not looking. They are the
people who seek to remove you from the position you occupy
so they can have it. They are the people who want to get you
fired at work because they are not happy with your excellent
performance. Jesus called King Herod a fox because he stole his
brother's wife.

"At that time, some Pharisees came to Jesus and
said to him, "Leave this place and go somewhere
else. Herod wants to kill you." [32] He replied, "Go
tell that fox, 'I will keep on driving out demons
and healing people today and tomorrow, and on
the third day I will reach my goal" (Luke 13:31-32
NIV).

Foxes will steal from you without a warning. They will steal
your ideas before you go ahead and execute them. They will
take money from you as a loan but will not repay you. Do not
be surprised when they act that way; they are only acting out
of their nature.

❖ The wolves

Wolves are those who come to be with you; they pretend to like you, but they do not; they come only because they seek to make you their prey. Wolves are the people who are with you only because they feed on you but care nothing about you. They will take advantage of you, use you for their profit, and dump you; they always leave when you are empty and have nothing more to give. Wolves are only after their own interests; they do not really care about you, even if they give the impression they do. Wolves come to be with you only to eat you dry. They are the people who will go to any length to betray, deceive, and even shed blood to make unjust gain.

> "Her officials within her are like wolves tearing their prey; they shed blood and kill people to make unjust gain" (Ezekiel 22:27 NIV)

Wolves are experts in disguise; they can disguise themselves to look like sheep easily. They will come in and try to blend in with the authentic ones, pretending to be with you and for you, but they are only there to use you for their own self-interest. Jesus says:

> "Beware of false prophets, which come to you in sheep's clothing, but inwardly they are ravening wolves" (Matthew 7:15 KJV).

Leaders who prey on the people and prophesy lies to manipulate them for their own benefit are wolves. There are many wolves out there, lying prophets who pose as gospel ministers and claim to have received a call from God, but they are ravening wolves who only have their stomachs' needs in mind. Paul the apostle warned about them in the book of Acts of the Apostles, saying:

> "Take heed therefore unto yourselves, and to all the flock, over which the Holy Ghost hath made you overseers, to feed the church of God, which he hath purchased with his own blood. [29] For I know this, that after my departing shall grievous wolves enter in among you, not sparing the flock" (Acts 20:28-29 KJV).

You need to pray for the gift of discernment of spirits to be operational in your life. You need God to open your eyes so you can see into the people who are around you and who you will encounter. Refuse to be a victim; Jesus said you will walk among them, and nothing will injure you. However, you must be able to identify wolves whenever you see them. You must operate in the power that Jesus gives and be victorious over them all.

CHAPTER 5

❦

THE GATES OF HELL, THE GATEWAY FOR EVIL SPIRITS

Satan is always looking for an opportunity to create loopholes, or openings, where he can have access to human beings and dominate them. Whenever Satan sees the opportunity, he uses it to create an opening, which is called the gates of hell. Satan's most important target is the believer in Christ, and he goes after him aggressively, like a roaring lion, according to the Bible.

> "Be alert and of sober mind. Your enemy the devil prowls around like a roaring lion looking for someone to devour" (1 Peter 5:8 NIV).

Satan is after the believer because, as it were, those who have not received Jesus as their Savior and Lord belong to his kingdom, and they are already easily accessible to him. The presence of believers anywhere in the world is Satan's greatest threat to his rulership and dominion on earth, so he targets them fiercely to dominate them and diminish their ability.

Satan has no authority over a believer; therefore, he cannot have any access to him unless the believer grants him the authority. When Satan gets the authority to have any access into a believer's life, he establishes what is called the gates of hell. The gates of hell are what give Satan unhindered access into believers' lives or affairs, and he can stand on their way and determine their wellbeing and welfare. Jesus speaks of the gates of hell in Matthew 16:18.

> "And I say also unto thee, That thou art Peter, and upon this rock I will build my church; and the gates of hell shall not prevail against it" (Matthew 16:18 KJV).

It is important to understand that hell is referring to Satan's kingdom or demonic power. For Satan's kingdom to succeed in accessing and influencing anyone's life, he must first establish the gates of hell. Wherever he succeeds in pitching the gates of hell, it will serve two purposes:

1) Firstly, the gates of hell create an opening or passage through which demons will freely enter a place, someone's life, or affairs to influence things or wreak havoc.

2) Secondly, the gates of hell would serve as a barrier, or blockade, for Satan. Satan will not only have free access to any place where he succeeded in establishing the gates of hell; he can also make the gates a blockade to anything good that God ordained for the person, holding the person back from advancing in life and standing on the way of his destiny.

Always remember that the gates of hell serve as Satan's pathway into someone's life and affairs, or as a blockade erected to prevent anything good from coming into someone's life. Satan uses the gates of hell to flood people's lives, homes, and affairs with demons and all kinds of evil at will. And since, through the gates of hell, Satan has unhindered access to people, he can also saturate their lives with things that appear to be good — the things that are not God's will for them —to take them off the plan and purpose of God. Do not allow Satan to succeed in erecting the gates of hell in your life. As you read the pages of this book, I decree and declare the collapse of the gates of hell, wherever they are in operation in your life, that Satan has pitched, in the mighty name of Jesus. Here are some of the circumstances that Satan capitalizes on to create the gates of hell. I share them with you so that you will give Satan no opportunity to use them to access your life. You must deal with them appropriately if they speak of your own personal life.

❖ Sinful lifestyle

Satan uses temptation to get people to fall into sin. Believers, especially, face temptation every day and everywhere. Temptation is the attraction to do what is contrary and against what God has said, and there is the opportunity created for it to happen. Satan does not tempt believers just for the sake of it. His drive is consistent: to steal, kill, and destroy. Sin creates an atmosphere that is not conducive to the Holy Spirit's work. The evil spirit will always flourish wherever the Holy Spirit is not allowed to work freely, which is what sin does.

Sin is antithetical to the operations of the Holy Spirit, and Satan knows that, so he wants people to live a life that is contrary and against what God said because he will always have a field day wherever sin is prevalent, and the Holy Spirit is not at work. A sin-filled environment is a condition conducive for demons to thrive. Satan is lethal where a sinful lifestyle is the order, but he is incapacitated where righteousness is the order.

Though sin does not necessarily make any believer cease from being a child of God, when a believer lives a sinful lifestyle, it opens his life up to demons' spirits, giving them the advantage to cause all kinds of havoc. Some sicknesses, diseases, and all kinds of problems and challenges come as consequences of a sinful lifestyle. Jesus revealed to a certain man that he healed from affliction, that his condition was because of his sinful lifestyle, and that worse things would happen to him if he went back to his sinful lifestyle.

> "Later Jesus found him at the temple and said to him, "See, you are well again. Stop sinning or something worse may happen to you" (John 5:14 NIV).

A sinful lifestyle can also cause the premature death of a believer. The death of a believer because of sin does not necessarily mean that the believer will go to hell. The price for sins was fully paid. However, a sinful lifestyle creates an opportunity for Satan to afflict the believer in the flesh.

> "It is actually reported that there is sexual immorality among you, and of a kind that even pagans do not tolerate: A man is sleeping with his father's wife. [5] hand this man over to Satan for

> the destruction of the flesh, so that his spirit may
> be saved on the day of the Lord." (1 Corinthians
> 5:1,5 NIV).

Satan gets to have the right to touch someone's flesh and may even cause the demise of the person if he gives himself to a lifestyle of sin. Sin is Satan's invention; you will come under his control if you embrace it.

> "Don't you know that when you offer yourselves
> to someone as obedient slaves, you are slaves of the
> one you obey-whether you are slaves to sin, which
> leads to death, or to obedience, which leads to
> righteousness?" (Romans 6:16 NIV).

You must always remember that Satan always has the upper hand against someone who is living in sin. Whoever makes sinning a lifestyle will become vulnerable to demons; they lord it over him, and they will succeed against him if they shoot their arrows at him, because it is only in righteousness that someone's safety from satanic attacks is guaranteed.

> "In righteousness shalt thou be established: thou
> shalt be far from oppression; for thou shalt not fear:
> and from terror; for it shall not come near thee"
> (Isaiah 54:14 KJV).

This is why a believer should not toy with sin or make excuses for sin. Avoiding sin is not only about not missing heaven. Whoever is in Christ has passed from death to life. Sin may not send a believer to hell. However, if he is living in sin, he will inevitably create a conducive environment around him for demons to fester. Demons are attracted to a sinful atmosphere;

they thrive there, and they will come in and erect the gates of hell in the place. No one who lives in wanton disregard for the word of God and His demand for living a holy life will be able to fight off demon spirits.

Understand that there is a difference between someone falling into sin and someone living a lifestyle of sin. A lifestyle of sin is when someone has normalized a sinful behavior and indulges in what is contrary to God's word. He knows that it is the wrong way to live, but he makes light of it. It is crucial that you are aware that it is the lifestyle of practicing sinful behavior that makes someone a slave and subject to Satan (Romans 6:16). Ensure that you are not trapped in it. Quickly get up and make it right with God when you are overtaken by temptation. Do not stay in it. There is forgiveness available for you; go to the Lord in repentance and receive cleansing through the blood of Jesus.

> "My dear children, I write this to you so that you will not sin. But if anybody does sin, we have an advocate with the Father-Jesus Christ, the Righteous One. [2] He is the atoning sacrifice for our sins, and not only for ours but also for the sins of the whole world" (1 John 2:1-2 NIV).

You must not make excuses for your sin or allow it to become a lifestyle. It is very dangerous for a believer to live life like that.

❖ Ignorance

Ignorance is a powerful tool Satan uses to have an advantage over people. Satan thrives in places where people are operating in ignorance of God's will. He will always capitalize on the ignorance of believers to take advantage of them. If Satan can get you to remain in ignorance, he will always be a step ahead of you. He has the advantage wherever the people are in the dark about what God said, what God's purpose is for them, what God is doing, or what their position is as the redeemed of Christ.

The believer's understanding of his position in Christ Jesus is very empowering and liberating. He is not going to be able to stand on his covenant rights and make a demand for them if he is ignorant of the covenant. Jesus says, "And ye shall know the truth, and the truth shall make you free" (John 8:32 KJV). Understanding of the truth of what God says will free the believer from bondage. However, ignorance makes the believer weak and powerless and places him at a disadvantage to Satan.

The Ignorance of the devices of Satan is especially very costly to a believer. If Satan can keep anyone in the dark about his activities and operations, he will be winning in his fight against the person. This is why the Bible says in 2 Corinthians 2:11, "Lest Satan should get an advantage of us: for we are not ignorant of his devices" (KJV). The importance of intelligence into an enemy's tools of war and strategy, to win a war, is substantial. This is why countries, irrespective of their military might, send out spies to spy against their potential enemies. They know that the intelligence into their enemy's strategy will give them an edge above them. The Holy Spirit is believers might, and their source of intelligence. The Holy Spirit gives believers understanding of hidden mysteries, He reveals to them the mind of God, and He reveals the schemes of Satan, to make believers more than a conqueror (John 16:13).

A believer who desires a winning streak must dedicate himself to studying the word of God to gain a deeper understanding of the ways of God, to develop himself spiritually, and to cultivate deep intimacy with the Holy Spirit. A deeper understanding of the word of God helps believers in their understanding of the leading of the Holy Spirit. The importance of understanding of the leading of the Holy Spirit and intimacy with Him cannot be overemphasised; it matters a great deal to a believer in his relationship with God and the actualization of His purpose. Ignorance has a powerful consequence; it can make someone lose connection with God and be separated from his or her inheritances in the kingdom of God. Bible says:

> "They are darkened in their understanding and separated from the life of God because of the ignorance that is in them due to the hardening of their hearts." (Ephesians 4:18 NIV).

An enemy who knows more will have the advantage. Ignorance is a menace. It keeps people in the dark; it separates people from what belongs to them; you can imagine how many people out there whose parents have died, leaving them an inheritance of great wealth, but unfortunately are not aware of it. They are potentially millionaires, but sadly, they are living in penury, not being able to meet their needs due to a lack of knowledge. What a tragedy! Ignorance is indeed extremely expensive. Ignorance makes people hardened; they foolishly insist on what is wrong and harmful to them due to their lack of understanding. It is like the case of a child who gets hold of a loaded gun, points it to his face and pulls the trigger. He lacks an understanding of its lethal effect due to ignorance.

There are many good people, including believers, who are suffering needlessly because of their ignorance. And that's why God said, "my people are destroyed from lack of knowledge……" (Hosea 4:6 NIV). You must reject ignorance as you would reject sin. Study to know everything you need to know. Give yourself to the study of the word daily. Create enough time for your time alone with God. Practice listening to the Holy Spirit and train yourself to understand Him.

❖ Negative confession

The words that we speak matter a lot in the grand scheme of things; they are powerful and creative, and they determine the daily occurrences in our lives. As huge as a ship is, it is only a tiny rudder that controls the direction it sails, and in such a way that even the waves of the sea yield to its power. The Bible shows us that, in the same way, the tongue possesses such a great power that it can impact the cause of our lives.

> "Or take ships as an example. Although they are so large and are driven by strong winds, they are steered by a very small rudder wherever the pilot wants to go. [5] Likewise, the tongue is a small part of the body, but it makes great boasts. Consider what a great forest is set on fire by a small spark. [6] The tongue also is a fire, a world of evil among the parts of the body. It corrupts the whole body, sets the whole course of one's life on fire, and is itself set on fire by hell" (James 3:4-6 NIV).

There are no idle words in the spirit realm; every word spoken will significantly impact your lives. Jesus says that whatever you say can either bring condemnation or justification.

> "But I tell you that everyone will have to give account on the day of judgment for every empty word they have spoken. [37] For by your words you will be acquitted, and by your words you will be condemned." (Matthew 12:36-37 NIV)

You must understand that what you say can either attract demon spirits or release the power of God. Words are creative; everything that you see came about through God's spoken words. Not through what they do but rather through the spoken word, humans are reborn and transformed. Hear what the Bible says regarding that:

> "For it is with your heart that you believe and are justified, and it is with your mouth that you profess your faith and are saved" (Romans 10:10 NIV).

Someone can have a demon-filled home because his talking point is all negative, sad, fearful, and worry-filled. Faith-filled words pull the Spirit of God, and His creative ability but negative talking attracts evil spirits. You must watch what you are saying about your life, your health, your marriage, your children, your career, your finances, etc. You put limitations on them, or you attract the anointing of the Holy Spirit to work on them, by what you are saying. Always note that if the things you say are contrary to God's word and are full of negativity, they carry negative consequences. However, if what you say lines up with God's word, it releases the creative power that is in God's word, and you will see what God said being fulfilled in your life. Never say my eye disease, my heart condition, my kind of headache, my this, my that, etc. They are not yours; they belong to the devil, so do not claim and own anything evil for yourself. You have got to reject it.

Do not make negative confessions, such as:

- ◆ Things are hard; I am fed up with life.
- ◆ It does not look like I am ever going to make it.
- ◆ I hate that person; I feel like killing him.
- ◆ I hate my job.
- ◆ I hate this country.
- ◆ I think something bad is going to happen.
- ◆ This exam I am writing is tough, and I am not sure I am going to make it.
- ◆ I am always having bad luck with relationships; I am bad luck.
- ◆ Why are things happening to me this way? I am cursed.
- ◆ This challenge is tough; it is going to kill me.
- ◆ This country is hard, and things are never going to get better.

Know that spirits, positive or negative, use what you say to effect changes in your physical world. So, the things you say will either give angels the tools to work with for you or give demons the tools to work with against you. You have to understand that as long as you keep making those unbelieving and negative confessions about you or the things you care about, you are never going to come out of the situations you are in because those confessions attract demons, and they give them the tools to work with them and birth the things you are saying.

Be aware that negative thoughts will come to your mind sometimes, and you cannot avoid them; nonetheless, ensure that you do not put them into words. Never utter the negative stuff that demons are whispering to you. Your situation may not be getting better; nonetheless, do not confess what the situation is; only say what you want to see. Do not speak out about how you feel; confess how you want to feel. The Bible says, let the weak say, I am strong (Joel 3:10).

❖ Bitterness, Envy, and strife

Satan will always have free access wherever there is bitterness, envy, and strife. That is one of the reasons why Satan will stir up trouble between brothers or sisters and create contention between them. He does that to sow bitterness and strife because they create a favorable environment for his demons. Anywhere there is house fighting, division, envying, and strife, you look closely, and you will notice that the people are not progressing; they will be experiencing all kinds of attacks; all kinds of sicknesses and diseases will be showing up in their midst; they will be having financial difficulties and hardships.

You must resist unhealthy competition amongst the brethren, it leads to envy, and it is destructive. Cain murdered his brother Abel out of envy (Genesis 4:3-8). Joseph's brothers sold him into Egypt for slavery out of envy (Genesis 37:1-28).

The Bible says, "For where envying and strife is, there is confusion and every evil work." (James 3:16 KJV). You must do your utmost to resist all forms of bitterness, learning to forgive completely from your heart. Bitterness and unforgiveness are dangerous; they are powerful tools that Satan uses to enter a place, and he holds people down and back. Satan is also aware that unforgiveness and keeping bitterness in your heart can make your prayer powerless. This is why Jesus says to ensure that you always forgive those who have sinned against you when you pray.

> "Therefore, I say unto you, What things soever ye desire, when ye pray, believe that ye receive them, and ye shall have them. [25] And when ye stand praying, forgive, if ye have ought against any: that your Father also which is in heaven may forgive you your trespasses. [26] But if ye do not forgive, neither will your Father which is in heaven forgive your trespasses" (Mark 11:24-26 KJV)

Jesus said, God will not forgive anyone who fails to forgive others, that have wrong him, and is holding bitterness against them. It is one thing to be praying a fervent prayer, but it is another thing for your prayer to be effectual, result yielding prayer. Your prayers will be powerless and ineffective if you hold bitterness. Also, bitterness and unforgiveness opens people's lives to tormentors; evil spirits that like to ruin things for people. According to Jesus the Heavenly Father Himself will hold back and allow the tormentors to afflict someone if he refuses to forgive.

> "Shouldest not thou also have had compassion on thy fellowservant, even as I had pity on thee? [34] And his lord was wroth, and delivered him to the tormentors, till he should pay all that was due unto him. [35] So likewise shall my heavenly Father do also unto you, if ye from your hearts forgive not

everyone his brother their trespasses" (Matthew 18:33-35 KJV).

The tormentors would come in the form of relationship wrecks, illnesses and diseases, financial ruins, and all kinds of calamities and misfortunes. The manifestation of the blessing of God is hindered and the anointing fails in an environment of bitterness and strife, where the people are not walking in love and forgiving one another.

> "How good and pleasant it is when God's people live together in unity! [2] It is like precious oil poured on the head, running down on the beard, running down on Aaron's beard, down on the collar of his robe. [3] It is as if the dew of Hermon were falling on Mount Zion. For there the LORD bestows his blessing, even life forevermore" (Psalm 133:1-3 NIV).

You must insist on unity in your home, between you and your spouse or your children. Insist on unity in your church. Pray against division, strife, and envy. They stand in the way of the anointing and create the right conditions for demons to fester.

❖ Disregard for Marital Covenant

When a couple disregards their marriage covenant and deals with each other out of contempt, they give Satan access to their marriage and home. Many believers are not aware that when they allow marital problems to persist, it can create a satanic gateway into their homes. Satan knows it, so he likes stirring up problems between husband and wife. He knows that, as the Bible has said, their prayers will be hindered because of that.

> "Wives, in the same way submit yourselves to your own husbands so that, if any of them do not believe the word, they may be won over without words by the behaviour of their wives" (1 Peter 3:1 NIV)

> "Husbands, in the same way be considerate as you live with your wives, and treat them with respect as the weaker partner and as heirs with you of the gracious gift of life, so that nothing will hinder your prayers." (1 Peter 3:7 NIV).

When couples ignore the marriage covenant and fail to deal with each other according to what the scripture says concerning marriage, their prayers are hindered. Think about it: who wins when your prayers are hindered? How does someone survive in this world if his prayers are not working? What becomes of his life —his health, his career, his children —where his prayers are meaningless? A believer's confidence in prayer is the fact that God answers prayers.

> "And this is the confidence that we have in him, that, if we ask anything according to his will, he heareth us" (1 John 5:14 KJV).

Prayers are useless if they do not move God. A believer is in the same situation as someone who does not know God and does not pray if his prayers are powerless and fail to yield any results.

❖ Disobedience

> "Wherein in time past ye walked according to the course of this world, according to the prince of the power of the air, the spirit that now worketh in the children of disobedience" (Ephesians 2:2 KJV)

There is a demon spirit that is the spirit of disobedience; it is among the demons operating within the level of spiritual wickedness in the heavenly realm. Everywhere you see disobedience, it is a manifestation of the presence of the prince of the power of the air. The disobedience spirit seeks to control people and influence them to walk in disobedience to any instituted authority, especially to God's law and command. Disobedience to God's law and command may come in the form of disobedience to the following, which God commanded that we obey:

- Disobedience to a clear leading of the Holy Spirit - Galatians 5:25
- Disobedience to Parents - Ephesians 6:1
- Disobedience to pastoral leadership - Hebrews 13:7,17
- Disobedience to Government authority - Romans 13:1-4; 1 Peter 2:13-14

There are people who hate anything authority; they resist any form of leadership; they hate being instructed or told what to do or not to do, and they will always rebel against it. God did not design man such that he would be independent of any authority figure in his life.

> "O LORD, I know that the way of man is not in himself: it is not in man that walketh to direct his steps" (Jeremiah 10:23 KJV).

You must understand that it is not ordinary; there are spirits of disobedience out there working in people, making them disobedient to all forms of authority. Here are three important things about disobedience you need to be aware of:

(I).   Disobedience is Satan's territory

The environment of disobedience is Satan's territory; he lives and functions in that domain. Satan is strong and powerful in his territory, and a believer has no chance of defeating him there, which is why the Bible says that a believer is not ready to avenge Satan until his obedience is complete.

> "And we will be ready to punish every act of disobedience, once your obedience is complete." (2 Corinthians 10:6 NIV).

You are not going to be able to punish demons by driving them out and putting a limitation on their operations if you are living in disobedience. In disobedience, you become vulnerable to demons. In disobedience, you are powerless against them. Engaging in a warfare prayer is dangerous for someone if he is not living holy and in obedience to God's word.

(II).   Disobedience stands on the way of a believer exercising their authority

Authority works on the principle of submission to an authority. No one can exercise authority legitimately if he is not under any form of authority. This is also a spiritual law; no one can exercise any authority over evil spirits and be able to cast them out if he is disobedient to the authority over him. This is why the Bible says believers are ready to avenge all disobedience only when their obedience is complete (2 Corinthians 10:6). Jesus marveled at a Roman centurion's understanding of how authority works, and he calls it much faith, the kind he has not seen in Israel:

> "For I also am a man subject to authority, with soldiers subject to me. And I say to one, Go, and he goes; and to another, Come, and he comes; and to my slave, do this, and he does it. [10] When Jesus heard him, He marveled and said to those who followed Him [who adhered steadfastly to Him, conforming to His example in living and, if need be, in dying also], I tell you truly, I have not found so much faith as this with anyone, even in Israel" (Matthew 8:9-10 AMPC).

Demons understand the spiritual law on which authority works, and to curtail someone's authority over them, they will get disobedient spirits to work hard to influence them and cage them in disobedience. Watch out, so you are not their victim.

(III). Disobedience stands on the way of believers' redemption benefits

A believer's salvation benefits may be curtailed, and he or she will not enjoy the abundant life that Jesus offers if they continue to live in disobedience to God. For Jesus to fully enforce salvation benefits in the life of any believer, he must learn to obey Jesus's teachings. Believers receive this understanding from the following scripture:

> "During the days of Jesus' life on earth, he offered up prayers and petitions with fervent cries and tears to the one who could save him from death, and he was heard because of his reverent submission. [8] Son though he was, he learned obedience from what he suffered [9] and, once made perfect, he became the source of eternal salvation for all who obey him". (Hebrews 5:7-9 NIV)

Jesus is the source of eternal salvation for all who obey him. Obedience to God is critical in the life of a believer. Ignoring God and refusing to do what He says to do is self-destructive. Obedience may cause a believer a lot; it may mean denying himself his civil rights and letting go of certain pleasures. However, when we obey God, He ensures that we enter and enjoy all the things that salvation entails in this physical world. Someone may be born again and still forfeit the benefits of salvation here on earth if he is ignoring God's word and living life in disrespect of God.

There are many believers who are suffering unnecessarily, and some have died because of it, not having actualized their blessing because they lived in disobedience. Is the Holy Spirit nudging you to do something? You heard Him clearly, but you are refusing to do what he is saying to do. I admonish you to go ahead and do whatever He says to you. Don't be afraid to do whatever He says to do. He will never lead you to harm. You may go through suffering in your obedience; however, in the long run, you will have a very powerful positive outcome. It really pays to obey God.

CHAPTER 6

SATAN'S DEVICES

"Lest Satan should get an advantage of us: for we are not ignorant of his devices" (2 Corinthians 2:11 KJV).

You must always remember that Satan has no power or authority over believers, and he cannot knock any believer down until the believer gives him a place in his life or let him get an advantage. You must also remember that one of the areas Satan gets an advantage and thrives in is people's ignorance, or where people deliberately choose to set aside their knowledge and walk contrary to what they know.

One of Satan's greatest strategies is to get the believer to walk in ignorance of his devices, because it gives him an advantage. Satan's devices refer to his schemes, methods of operation, the tricks he uses, and his weapons of warfare. Satan does not want you to know when he is coming against you, how, where, or what tool he is employing.

Satan uses many devices in his operation; he uses material things, he comes in the spirit realm, he uses people, he comes looking like an angel, etc. It is important that you are not ignorant, whichever way he comes and whatever tool he chooses to make use of; he will have an advantage over you if you are ignorant. I will share with you some of Satan's devices however, they are not exclusive. It is important that you study the scriptures in order to understand it. It is important that you develop relationship with the Holy Spirit, so that you can understand His leading in your life. It is important also that you pray for the gift of discernment of spirits to operate in your life, so that you will be acutely aware anytime Satan is seeking to infiltrate your domain.

Devoting yourself to sufficient time for the study of the word of God and maintaining a vibrant prayer life will help tremendously to keep you spiritually alert. A lot of believers get overtaken, and they fall victims of Satan's devices easily because they are spiritually shallow, unaware, spiritually cold, not fervent in spirit, and more carnally minded.

❖ Satan's stay back trick

The stay-back trick is Satan's way of keeping people away from where God wants them to be at a particular given time, and by doing so, he keeps them away from their help, from encountering God, and from receiving their blessing. It is important to understand that there is a time for everything under the sun and that God does His things at the right time.

> "There is a time for everything, and a season for every activity under the heavens" (Ecclesiastes 3:1 NIV)

> "He has made everything beautiful in its time. He
> has also set eternity in the human heart; yet no one
> can fathom what God has done from beginning to
> end" (Ecclesiastes 3:11 NIV).

It is important to know and work with God's timing. Many people will finish as underachievers in this world, not because they lack the ability to achieve remarkable success but because they do not understand the importance of timing. If you do not understand timing, you will ruin the process of birthing your destiny and hinder its manifestation. To operate outside of timing is the same as someone who is trying to bring out a baby from the mother's womb when the pregnancy is only three months old; that would make it an abortion, because the child will not survive. The Bible says:

> "I returned, and saw under the sun, that the race
> is not to the swift, nor the battle to the strong,
> neither yet bread to the wise, nor yet riches to
> men of understanding, nor yet favour to men of
> skill; but time and chance happeneth to them all"
> (Ecclesiastes 9:11 KJV).

Know that whenever it is God's timing for you to step into something new, He will create the chance or opportunity for you. Your chances to breakthrough and advance in life is linked with your ability to key in and press in at the right time. It is self-sabotaging to understand the right time for you to do something and ignore it. This is why it is significantly important to understand and to follow the leading of the Holy Spirit, and to learn to do whatever He says to do.

Never allow Satan to keep you back from the place that you ought to be. He will create reasons and excuses for you not to go to the place you are meant to be. Do not stay back watching TV when you should be in church, or at a prayer meeting. Never allow the devil to keep you away from your assignment. Do not go late to interviews. Do everything possible to remember appointment. Satan was able to present Bathsheba to David because he stayed back, at the time that kings should be at the war front. And he brought calamity to David's house (2 Samuel 11: 1-5). If Satan can dislocate you, he can make you disabled. Do not let Satan separate you from the people you are meant to be with. If he can isolate you, he can annihilate you. Do not stay back when you need to be somewhere else.

Satan will want to use procrastination against you. Do not say I will go tomorrow when you should go today. One important principle of life is to learn to do what you need to do today, because you may not get another chance to do it. Any time you spend is part of the time apportioned to you to spend here on earth, and you will never have it back. It is possible that if you do not do what you are meant to do today, you may never get the time or the opportunity to do it again.

❖ Satan's it does not matter trick

The things you think do not matter may be especially important in the scheme of things. Satan wants you to trivialize important things —things that will impact your destiny. Satan uses things that appear harmless to ruin many destinies. Things that may ruin someone may not necessarily be sinful, but they have the capacity to become controlling and harmful to the person. What you think does not matter can eventually become a monster. This is why Paul the apostle admonishes:

> "All things are lawful unto me, but all things are not expedient: all things are lawful for me, but I will not be brought under the power of any"
> (1 Corinthians 6: 12 KJV)

That drug addiction started because of one puff, which a friend said would not matter; it was just a one-off, you thought, but alas, it became the first of many. Someone may argue that alcohol is not a sin, but it can lead to addiction, rob someone of their finances, ruin their career, destroy relationships, and lead to high blood pressure, heart disease, stroke, liver disease, digestive problems, cancer of the breast, mouth, throat, oesophagus, voice box, liver, colon, and rectum. What you think does not matter can become the monster that will ruin you. You must learn to keep away from anything that has the potential to trap you and ruin you.

You may think that it does not matter that you are living together with your fiancé, and you say we are going to get married soon. And you may think that there is nothing wrong with kissing and cuddling each other if you do not have sex, but there is everything wrong with it. It can lead to sex and pregnancy before marriage, and you will be forfeiting the marriage blessing that awaits you. You may think that there is nothing wrong with a believer dating an unbeliever, but there is everything wrong with it. You may end up in a marriage with a person who is a child of the devil and have Satan as your father-in-law. You may think that there is nothing wrong with going to a nightclub if you are not going to join your friends to do what is not appropriate for a believer to do. However, it may only be a matter of time, and you will end up joining them.

You must be careful with what Satan is saying 'it does not really matter'. As a believer, the thing that should matter to you is what the Word of God says and the way the Holy Spirit is leading you. You may think it does not matter; however, you need to listen to your spirit. You may not understand why the Spirit is leading you otherwise, but if your spirit troubles you about something, you should listen. Yes, it may not appear sinful, but know that He will not mislead you to what has no baring to your destiny.

❖ Satan's nobody will know trick

Satan uses nobody will know tricks, especially to keep people bound in unhealthy habits and secret sin. It really does not matter whether someone knows about the things you do or not. Everything you do comes with consequences, whether they are known to people or not. The law of seedtime and harvest applies to all aspects of human life. It works in spiritual things and in material things because it is both a natural law and a spiritual law. And it impacts human relationships as well. Therefore, there will be a harvest from everything you do, whether it is done secretly or in the open.

> "Therefore, all things whatsoever ye would that men should do to you, do ye even so to them: for this is the law and the prophets" (Matthew 7:12 KJV).

So do not fall for Satan's lies; that after all, no one will know. You can secretly do things to harm others, but then you will eventually reap the harvest of your deeds. You may secretly compromise your standing with God and do things that are not appropriate for you to do. Do not deceive yourself into thinking that no one will know, and so it does not matter. God, who sees everything we do, whether in secret or in the open, is the one we have to do with; he is the rewarder, not human beings.

> "Neither is there any creature that is not manifest in his sight: but all things are naked and opened unto the eyes of him with whom we have to do" (Hebrews 4:13 KJV).

In the life of a believer, what should count the most is how God sees him and not people's impression. (2 Corinthians 5:9). Dishonoring God in secret while making a show of piousness in the open is a hypocritical and self-defeating lifestyle. People may not approve of the things you do, but it is okay if God approves of them. A believer must not be a man-pleaser but a God-pleaser. He must not be an eye-service man, but someone who serves God with the sincerity of his heart.

> "Not with eyeservice, as men pleasers; but as the servants of Christ, doing the will of God from the heart; [7] With good will doing service, as to the Lord, and not to men" (Ephesians 6:6-7 KJV).

You will become a victim of Satan's 'no one will know trick,' if you are more concerned about how people see you than how God sees you. Know that it does not really matter the pedestal people have placed you, if God has not approved of you, you are nothing. You may appear holy, important, and powerful before people, but you will be the least in the sight of God, if your lifestyle does not honour Him. You can deceive people, but you can never deceive God. People may never get to know your secret life but God with whom we have to do, sees all things (Hebrews 4:13). Do not get trapped in secret sin; He who sees in secrets rewards openly (Matthew 6:1-8).

❖ Satan's everybody is doing it trick

Satan wants you to think that because everyone is going to it, it makes it okay. However, it does not work like that with God. The fact that everyone is doing something does not mean that God approves of it. Not even if the person who does it is a minister of the gospel that you hold in high esteem. Moreover, God deals with and relates to us individually, so you must figure out for yourself the path God has ordained for you. As a follower of Jesus, you must not be a crowd follower; you must know for yourself what the Word of God says and what God is saying for you to do as an individual. It is important that you understand that, because the fact that everybody is doing something does not make it right. Also, just because someone did something and got away with it does not mean that he did what was right and God approves of his behavior.

Someone may do something and get away with it, while someone else will do the same thing and bear severe consequences. That some people are not living right with God and they are 'prospering' or seem to be manifesting 'the power of God' in their lives and ministries should not make you envious of them or make you copy what they are doing. What you see manifesting may not really be the manifestation of the power of God, and their prosperity may be Satan's deception to make their lifestyle appear immaterial and inconsequential. That some men of God have divorced their wives and gone ahead to remarry a few days later does not mean that God approves of divorce; it does not change the way God sees divorce. The Bible says,

> "The man who hates and divorces his wife," says the Lord, the God of Israel, "does violence to the one he should protect," says the Lord Almighty. So be on your guard, and do not be unfaithful" (Malachi 2:16 NIV).

Know God for yourself. Do not follow the crowd; walk with God. Stick to the word, irrespective of what you see others doing, and it does not matter how anointed or powerful they claim to be. It is okay to stand alone if you are standing with God. Standing with God makes one a majority. Be happy to stand alone if you must; you will be the majority!

❖ Satan's God is merciful and will understand trick

Satan is a liar; do not give him the chance to preach the gospel to you. Satan quotes scripture only when he seeks an advantage. God is merciful and will indeed always forgive any wrongdoing. There is absolutely nothing that God cannot forgive. However, God's forgiveness does not always remove the consequences of our actions here on earth. Certain things that we do will leave us with indelible marks. Satan is after the mark it will leave on us, and he will use it to serve his purpose. For instance, the fact that God will forgive someone of sexual sin may still not protect him from the affliction of certain sexual diseases that may come on him because of his actions, or he may have a child out of wedlock, and God will not stand in the way of a pregnancy occurring.

Yes, God will be merciful and forgive anyone who steals. However, God will not protect the thief from getting caught, from being convicted, and from being sent to prison. Satan very much knows about God's grace and forgiveness, but he is also aware of the consequences of certain lifestyles or actions that forgiveness may not undo. The mercy of God notwithstanding, Satan knows that he can use the results of a believer's disobedience to tarnish his reputation, weaken the power of his witness, and curtail his impact in life.

The story of the young son, whom we refer to as the prodigal son, in Luke chapter 15:11-32 is a good example for us here. The young son asked the father for his own part of the inheritance; he got it and left home for a faraway country. In the new country, the Bible records that he squandered everything he had on wanton living and on prostitutes. He returned home to his father after he had squandered everything he had. The father received him back, forgave him, and threw a party for his welcome. However, his father's forgiveness did not undo his wasteful life; it did not restore his inheritance, which he wasted. When the older son complained about the father's forgiveness of the younger son, the father's reply to him was very revealing:

> "My son,' the father said, 'you are always with me, and everything I have is yours. [32] But we had to celebrate and be glad, because this brother of

yours was dead and is alive again; he was lost and is
found" (Luke 15:31-32 NIV).

Everything the father had remaining belonged to the older son
as his inheritance. The younger son would still have to pay
for the consequences of his reckless and wasteful living. The
father's mercy did not bring back his inheritance, which he had
squandered; he may now have to live on his brother's goodwill
and generosity. God's forgiveness does not set aside the law of
seedtime and harvest. The Bible says,

> "Do not be deceived: God is not mocked, for
> whatever one sows, that will he also reap. [8] For
> the one who sows to his own flesh will from the
> flesh reap corruption, but the one who sows to
> the Spirit will from the Spirit reap eternal life"
> (Galatians 6:7-8 ESV).

No one can mock God, no one should indulge in something
that God abhors because he says God is a forgiving God.
God forgives sins but He does not overlook it. God will be an
uncaring father if He overlooks sin and does not chastise his
children for their wrong actions. Chastisement is not indicative
of unforgiveness, but rather, a loving care (Hebrews 12:7).
You may not be able to avoid certain consequences, Satan
knows it, and that is why he will want to use the mercy of
God and forgiving nature to trick you into doing something.
Furthermore, the Bible says, "what shall we say then? Shall we
continue in sin, that grace may abound"? (Romans 6:1 KJV).
It is foolish to capitalise on the grace of God and carry-on
sinning.

CHAPTER 7

YOUR VICTORY OVER
EVIL SPIRITS

"Finally, my brethren, be strong in the Lord and in the power of His might. [11] Put on the whole armor of God, that you may be able to stand against the wiles of the devil. [12] For we do not wrestle against flesh and blood, but against principalities, against powers, against the rulers of the darkness of this age, against spiritual hosts of wickedness in the heavenly places" (Ephesians 6: 10-12 KJV)

We are in a constant battle against Satan's kingdom. He has unleashed on us his evil spirits, and they are seeking to infiltrate every aspect of human existence and bring it under their control. Satan's forces are bombarding us on every side with intensity, and they are more aggressive than ever because they realize that they do not have much time before the return of our Savior, Jesus Christ. They are attacking relationships; they are attacking marriages, they are attacking people's health, careers, finances, and their children. Satan's goal is to overthrow people's faith in God. He wants people to become disillusioned with God, be spiritually weak, and walk away from the faith.

Satan will continue his attack unrelentingly until he establishes his reign; however, he is not going to be victorious over those who have given their lives to Jesus, who are saved, and who enjoy a robust relationship with God. The commitment of one's life to Jesus and becoming born again is critical for achieving victory over evil spirits. The Bible says:

> "For everyone born of God overcomes the world. This is the victory that has overcome the world, even our faith. [5] Who is it that overcomes the world? Only the one who believes that Jesus is the Son of God" (1 John 5:4-5 NIV).

There is no victory outside of a relationship with Jesus. People need Jesus to overcome the onslaught of evil forces.

> "But thanks be to God! He gives us the victory through our Lord Jesus Christ" (1 Corinthians 15:57 NIV).

Anyone who is not born of God belongs in the kingdom of Satan, and Satan can dominate and manipulate him for his purpose anytime he chooses. However, being born again delivers individuals from the kingdom and authority of Satan, placing them in the kingdom of Jesus.

> "And giving joyful thanks to the Father, who has qualified you to share in the inheritance of his holy people in the kingdom of light. [13] For he has rescued us from the dominion of darkness and

brought us into the kingdom of the Son he loves"
(Colossians 1:12-13 NIV).

To be a born-again person is important; it elevates the believer
to be seated with Christ, far above principalities and powers
(Ephesians 1:17-23). Furthermore, the believer in Christ must
also live and walk by faith to sustain their position in Christ
Jesus.

> "Now the just shall live by faith: but if any man
> draws back, my soul shall have no pleasure in him.
> [39] But we are not of them who draw back unto
> perdition; but of them that believe in the saving of
> the soul" (Hebrews 10:38-39 KJV).

> "For whatsoever is born of God overcometh the
> world: and this is the victory that overcometh the
> world, even our faith" (1 John 5:4 KJV).

Living by faith means ordering your life and your affairs
according to the dictates of the word of God. It means to
trust in God, to hold His word dear, to see yourself in the
light of what God's word says, and to do what it says to do.
Satan's primary target against the believer is his faith. Satan
knows that the believer can live in victory over his demons only
when he lives by faith. Satan may attack the believer's welfare
and wellbeing; however, the goal has never been the physical
wellbeing of the believer but his spiritual wellbeing. He knows
that if he can touch the believer's faith, he will be able to keep
him down, hold him back, and sabotage his destiny.

As a believer, you must maintain a healthy and robust
spiritual life. You cannot afford to become a sleepy believer.

Sleepy believers are Christians who are not passionate about the things of God; their love for God is cold, and they take spiritual things lightly. Sleepy believers are those who spend most of their time with unbelievers; they do not talk to them about Jesus, and they are comfortable with it. Their prayer life is dull and sporadic. They stay away from church meetings, and it does not bother them.

Also, sleepy believers are more interested in material things than in the things of God. They can easily compromise their standing with God for worldly gain. They can easily tell lies and take advantage of other people for what they can have and enjoy in this world, and their conscience is seared about it; they are never convicted whatsoever (1 Timothy 4:2). They are struggling with unhealthy habits. They make excuses for their sinful behavior. According to scripture, for anyone to stand against the wiles of the devil, they must become strong in the Lord.

> "Finally, my brethren, be strong in the Lord, and in the power of his might. [11] Put on the whole armour of God, that ye may be able to stand against the wiles of the devil" (Ephesians 6: 10-11 KJV).

A believer who is strong in the Lord has healthy spiritual wellbeing. He is someone who enjoys a sound, fervent, and consistent prayer life. He has discovered the nourishing power of the word of God and is devoted to studying it. He is living in holiness. Furthermore, he dedicates himself to prayer and fasting. Every believer needs to live a life of prayer and fasting. Fasting helps the believer to focus on God and to concentrate more on spiritual things than the things of the world. You will observe that the believer who commits to fasting is gaining power over unhealthy habits or the besetting sins he struggles with. He is being faithful to God with his money; he consistently gives to fund the gospel and to meet the needs of the saints.

1 Corinthians 10: 1-13 gives us the example of people who started out well with God but who did not end well. The scripture shows that their faith was overthrown, and their destiny was destroyed because they fell out of fellowship with God and walked in unbelief. Their story was told in the scripture for our admonition, with the intent that we would learn from their mistakes and not walk in their footsteps of unbelief.

To live a victorious Christian life, there are important principles from the word of God you must understand and abide by. I present to you four principles that can help you walk in victory wherever you are:

❖ The <u>Take heed</u> principle

> "Wherefore let him that thinketh he standeth take
> heed lest he fall" (1 Corinthians 10: 12 KJV).

It is critical that you understand that no human being has ever passed the point of not being able to fall, no matter how high he rises spiritually. Anyone can fall from grace, irrespective of how high they have risen. And Satan is working hard to bring down standing and firebrand believers. To avoid falling, as the scripture instructed, he who is standing must take heed. To take heed means to pay attention, to watch out, to be on guard, or to be cautious. The first thing to watch out for and pay attention to is to constantly remember that you are human, that you are not sufficient on your own, and that you need God to survive life. On your own, you cannot overcome Satan.

> "Not that we are sufficient of ourselves to think anything of ourselves; but our sufficiency is of God" (2 Corinthians 3:5 KJV).

You must remember and never forget that you can only stand by the grace of God. The day you forget that you are a mere human and can fall, and you need to trust in God to uphold you, that very day will mark the beginning of your descent because you are not sufficient for yourself. You are not a superhero by yourself and not a giant before the devil, but only a sinner saved by the grace of God. You must never forget that it can only take the help of God, who saved you, for you to stand and not fall. You cannot rely on your own strength. The Bible says:

> 'Now all glory to God, who is able to keep you from falling away and will bring you with great joy into his glorious presence without a single fault" (Jude 1:24 NLT).

If you can remember that you need God to see you through, it will help you not lean on or depend on your capability or strength. You won't neglect the place of prayer; prayer is a powerful way that we demonstrate our reliance on God and trust in His help every step of the way. Trusting God is what the scripture says to do.

"Trust in the Lord with all thine heart; and lean not unto thine own understanding. [6] In all thy ways acknowledge him, and he shall direct thy paths. [7] Be not wise in thine own eyes: fear the Lord and depart from evil" (Proverbs 3:5-7 KJV).

You must have humility and never feel holier than thou, especially on the occasion of someone's fall or defeat, and go about making a quick judgement before understanding their circumstances. Take heed that you do not develop an invincible attitude. Your attitude towards those who are overtaking in fault and are down, especially, reveals your understanding of God's grace. You, who are standing, are standing by the grace of God. The Bible says:

"Brethren, if a man be overtaken in a fault, ye which are spiritual, restore such a one in the spirit of meekness; considering thyself, lest thou also be tempted" (Galatians 6:1. KJV).

Take heed that you do not fall, no matter how high you have risen, and watch out for Satan's attacks whenever you get involved in the restoration of someone who has fallen.

❖ The <u>Do not look back</u> principle

"Another said, "Yes, Lord, I will follow you, but first let me say good-bye to my family. [62] But Jesus told him, "Anyone who puts a hand to the plow and then looks back is not fit for the Kingdom of God" (Luke 9: 61-62 NLT).

The kingdom of God refers to God's will for you, the destiny He has in store for you, and your inheritance in Christ Jesus. We are all on our journey to the place God is seeking to take us, and it is those who are not going to look back who will reach their destiny. Jesus said anyone who looks back is not fit for the kingdom.

One of Satan's greatest strategies for making believers forfeit what God has for them and lose their destiny is by getting them to look back. No one who looks back can make steady headway forward. To go forward, you need to put your past behind you. Nobody really makes any meaningful or considerable progress with his eyes behind him; he will only stumble and fall. If you are looking back, you will eventually stumble and fall; it will only be a matter of time before it happens.

> "No, dear brothers and sisters, I am still not all I should be, but I am focusing all my energies on this one thing: Forgetting the past and looking forward to what lies ahead, [14] I strain to reach the end of the race and receive the prize for which God, through Christ Jesus, is calling us up to heaven" (Philippians 3: 13-14 NLT).

There are certain things, certain jobs, or even relationships that are in your past that you must close the door of your life against. You cannot go back to them because you are aware that they always hold you back. You must be willing to let go of anything in your past that is pulling you backward. Until you sever its influence over you, you are not going to progress; Satan is going to use it against you. Even Jesus was able to accomplish his goal and is now sitting at the right hand of God, the Father, because He was focused on the joy that was before Him and did not allow the things he suffered to distract Him (Hebrews 12: 1-3). Here are three things that can be present in everyone's past that have the potential to impact his or her journey going forward.

♦ Guilt

We all have a past, and there could be things there that we like to forget because we feel guilty when we recall them. Guilt has the potential to affect one's confidence and creativity. Satan is aware of that, and that is why he will not want you to forget certain things in your past that are horrible or that you are ashamed of. The Bible calls him the accuser of the brethren. He is an expert at reminding people of their mistakes to hold them back.

You may not be able to go forward if Satan can keep you focusing on the abortion you had, on the reckless life you lived, or on the failed relationship you have had. Satan knows that if he can get you to focus on your past, you may not forgive yourself, you may wallow in guilt, you may feel deficient, you may wallow in bitterness, and you may not fight for what you have ahead of you. Satan wants you to feel unworthy, like a failure, and to quit. You cannot quit because God has no record of anything in your past that was contrary to you. He took it and hung it with Jesus on the cross.

> "You were dead because of your sins and because your sinful nature was not yet cut away. Then God made you alive with Christ. He forgave all our sins. [14] He canceled the record that contained the charges against us. He took it and destroyed it by nailing it

to Christ's cross. [15] In this way, God disarmed the
evil rulers and authorities. He shamed them publicly
by his victory over them on the cross of Christ"
(Colossians 2: 13-15 NLT).

Furthermore, Satan knows that if you hold onto your past, you
are not going to make a fresh start, you will not find happiness,
and you will not find enjoyment and fulfilment in what is in
your present. You must forgive what is in your past. Accept
God's forgiveness and forgive yourself as well. Forgive everyone
who hurt you along the way. Make your mind up to move
forward and make a fresh start. Your best days are ahead of
you, not at the place you are coming from.

♦ Enticement and temptation

You are where you are today because you let go of many things.
You made such sacrifices even though the things you left
were precious to you, but you wanted something that meant
more, and you knew that unless you let them go, you could
not move forward. Satan will try to show you the things you
left, reminding you of what you are missing, tempting you
to go back. You should not look back, because if you do, you
could be tempted to return to them. Do not allow yesterday's
pleasures to ruin the wonderful things that are before you.
Satan will remind you of 'the good old days.' He will show you
the women, men, money, alcohol, and recognition and prestige
you "enjoyed," luring you to go back to where you came from.

The times that you will be most vulnerable are when things are
getting difficult and rough for you. But you must remember
Lot's wife and be prepared to walk away.

> "Remember what happened to Lot's wife! [33]
> Whoever clings to this life will lose it, and whoever
> loses this life will save it" (Luke 17: 32-33 NLT).

Your Christian life is never going to be smooth and easy-going. Things do not always happen the way we want them to, not necessarily because that God abandoned us, because we have sinned and are reaping the consequences of it, or because we are in the wrong place. God allows us to go through certain experiences —experiences that are not of His making — because He knows that their outcome will be for our own good.

> "For our present troubles are quite small and
> won't last very long. Yet they produce for us an
> immeasurably great glory that will last forever!
> [18] So we don't look at the troubles we can see
> right now; rather, we look forward to what we
> have not yet seen. For the troubles we see will
> soon be over, but the joys to come will last forever"
> (2 Corinthians 4: 17- 18 NLT).

Satan will use your challenges to make you think you are missing something beautiful as a Christian. He wants you to think that the Christian life is not worth the pain, the suffering, and the sacrifice you are making. He wants you to think that where you are coming from is better. Do not let him use your past to stand in the way of what God has in stock for you now and in the future.

> "And truly, if they had been mindful of that
> country from whence they came out, they might
> have had the opportunity to have returned. [16]
> But now they desire a better country, that is, an

heavenly: wherefore God is not ashamed to be called their God: for he hath prepared for them a city" (Hebrews 11:15-16 KJV).

You must go to God in prayer, seeking grace and help, especially when you notice that your mind likes going back to the things you have left behind. Don't let your mind fixate on them; the mind is powerful. Fix it on the beautiful things that God is working out in your future.

♦ Past glory

There are many people who are so engrossed in their past glory that they cannot see the new things God wants to do through them. Passed glory, if focused on, will steal your vision and make you lose touch with God, such that you will not experience the present move of God. Many people like to talk about their past conquests to prove their relevance; however, God is also the God of new things.

> "Remember ye not the former things, neither consider the things of old. [19] Behold, I will do a new thing; now it shall spring forth; shall ye not know it? I will even make a way in the wilderness, and rivers in the desert" (Isaiah 43:18-19 KJV).

Your yesterday's achievement and success are not your limit; there is still a lot before you to achieve. Do not let the devil use your yesterday's trophies to blind you to the greater things awaiting you. What is in your past is nothing compared to where God wants to take you. Your yesterday is history; your present is necessary; but the future must be your goal. Do not stay in your past glory.

❖ The <u>Give no place to the devil</u> principle

> "Neither give place to the devil" (Ephesians 4: 27 (KJV).

To give the devil no place means to not allow him to have any opportunity, or a loophole. Remember, if you are born again, Satan has no right over you and cannot touch you or anything that is yours unless you give him the opportunity. Satan is always going around as a roaring lion, looking for someone he can devour. He can only devour the people he has an advantage over.

> "Be sober, be vigilant; because your adversary the devil, as a roaring lion, walketh about, seeking whom he may devour" (1 Peter 5:8 KJV).

As the devil goes all over the place, all he is looking for in anybody's life is an opportunity. Do not give him the opportunity. Here are some of the circumstances that, when you let them happen, will create an opportunity and give Satan a chance to infiltrate your life.

- ♦ **A prayerless life.** That is why Jesus says to watch and pray so that you do not fall (Matthew 27:41).

- ♦ **Being unequally yoked.** Going into a relationship with an unbeliever is like putting fire under your bosom and expecting not to get burned. It is only a matter of time, and you would start compromising your relationship with God (2 Corinthians 6:24; Proverbs 6:27). You will have to avoid making people whose lifestyle you do not want to impact yours become your closest friends. The life of the people you spend the most time with will eventually rob on you (1 Corinthians 15:33).

♦ **Accepting inappropriate gifts**. Gifts blind the eyes and influences decisions. Be careful with the gifts you receive and from whom they come from. Many gifts are bribes and they are given to have access to your heart and influence your decision (proverbs 15:27; proverbs 29:4).

♦ **Tasting the apple when you do not want to eat it**. This is especially important for young and unmarried believers who desire to live holy, maintain their chastity, and keep away from sex until marriage. You will need to watch how you date. If you start touching, playing with your sensitive areas, and staying overnight, you are creating the space for demons to invade your relationship and control it.

♦ **Wrong places**. The places you frequently go are indicative of your inner struggles. Avoiding these places will prevent you from being lured and taken captive by evil spirits. For instance, if you do not want to watch porn, do not go to porn sites; if you do not want to drink, do not spend time in the pub; if you do not want to sleep with a whore, do not visit a brothel. Ask yourself, what is pulling me there? If you can stay away, you can beat it.

❖ The <u>Flee from or Keep away</u> principle

Believers are fighters, not quitters. You must learn to stand your ground when you must. You do not run away from demons; you are to stand your ground and resist them in the name of Jesus, and they will flee before you (James 4:8). However, there are a few things God has said we are not to confront and to flee from whenever they confront us. Staying and confronting them will be a self-defeating exercise because it will go against what God said to do. Fleeing from them is God's way of becoming victorious over them; you should not rebuke them or cast them out; the only way to fight and overcome them is to keep away from them. Here are some four things that God said to flee from:

♦ All appearance of evil -

> "Abstain from all appearance of evil"
> (1 Thessalonians 5: 22 KJV).

You must learn to keep away from anything that appears to you as evil, and it does not matter whether it is evil or not. If it seems to you to be evil, avoid it. A sin can be anything that, to you, is a wrong or inappropriate thing to do. It is a sin for you to go ahead and do what is not acceptable or appropriate for you.

> "If anyone, then, knows the good they ought to do and doesn't do it, it is sin for them" (James 4:17 NIV).

You should obey your conscience; it will always point you to what is right or wrong, or what is acceptable to God for you.

> "This is how we know that we belong to the truth and how we set our hearts at rest in his presence: [20] If our hearts condemn us, we know that God is greater than our hearts, and he knows everything. [21] Dear friends, if our hearts do not condemn us, we have confidence before God" (1 John 3:19-21 NIV).

Always stand down and walk away when your conscience condemns you, and it really does not matter who else is doing the thing. Something that can be harmful to you may not be harmful to another person. Do not let anyone convince you to do something that your heart does not accept; refrain from getting involved until you are convinced about it.

♦ Youthful lust

> "Run from anything that stimulates youthful lust. Follow anything that makes you want to do right. Pursue faith and love and peace and enjoy the companionship of those who call on the Lord with pure hearts." (2Tim. 2: 22 NLT).

Youthful lust is speaking of those cravings that are typical of young people, which, if not put in check, can take them off course and ruin their lives. There are quite a few things that are tempting to young people, some of which include the longing for acceptance, and this can lead them to compromise their values or be involved with the wrong people. There are many young people whose uncontrolled desire for acceptance has completely changed the trajectory of their lives. They got into trouble with the law and ended up in prison because they wanted to belong in a group. Knowing you are accepted by God, irrespective of what anyone thinks, and loving yourself and feeling good about who you are, is an immensely powerful feeling. Feeling this way will give one the boldness and confidence to face life and walk into the future.

Another form of youthful lust is the uncontrolled longing for pleasure. Many young people get trapped by it, and as a result, they go for all kinds of parties and entertainments, including road trips, drinking, and orgies, and they get into all sorts of inappropriate behaviour, the consequences of which can be damaging. The Bible teaches that loving the world, the things in it, and the pleasure of life is not of God.

> "Do not love the world or anything in the world. If anyone loves the world, love for the father is not in them. [16] For everything in the world- the lust of the flesh, the lust of the eyes, and the pride of life-comes not from the father but from the world. [17] The world and its desires pass away, but whoever does the will of God lives forever" (1 John 2:15-17 NIV).

According to James, sometimes the prayers of believers are not being answered because they are being driven by their lust.

> "Ye ask, and receive not, because ye ask amiss, that ye may consume it upon your lusts" (James 4:3 KJV).

Praying to God while motivated by one's lust does not yield any result whatsoever. God cares about us. God wants to answer our prayers and meet our needs. However, He does not want believers to be more concerned about satisfying their pleasures than living a purposeful life. I went into farming at the age of 22, and I was full of faith that God was going to use it to bless me and make me a millionaire. I believed that I was going to build my mansion before I get to age 25, buy me a Mercedes Benz, and marry a very pretty lady, and together we would enjoy life. I fasted and prayed over the farm for a great increase. However, nothing came out of the farm. During one of my evening visits to the farm, a black cobra almost bit me. My attention was drawn to the reptile a few steps before placing my foot within its reach because of its hissing sound. I believe I would have died alone on the farm that day. The farm was far away from the highway, and I was there alone. That evening visit was my last visit to the farm.

Looking back, I can tell now that my fasting and prayer did not yield the result I hoped for because I was driven by my lust. I went into farming because of my pride and craving for material wealth. I did not pay attention to what the will of God is for me. God had other plans for me. It was not long after that experience that I heard the call of God to enrol in missions and get trained in a mission school. My training in the school of missions played a significant role in bringing me to where I am today.

A believer's life should not just be about what they can have and enjoy. The Bible says a man's life consists not in the abundance of the things he possesses (Luke 12:15). Believers must also prioritize the needs of others and make themselves available for

God to use them as a blessing. In Jesus's parable of the sower, He shows us that the effect of the word of God in people's lives diminishes, and the word does not bear any fruits, if the people who hear the word give themselves more to the cares of this world and are after pleasure.

> "This is the meaning of the parable: The seed is the word of God. [14] The seed that fell among thorns stands for those who hear, but as they go on their way they are choked by life's worries, riches, and pleasures, and they do not mature" (Luke 8:11,14 NIV).

Satan knows that he can choke the word of God in you and make it not bear fruit if he can get you to lust after pleasure and the cares of life. The youth also face challenges with their appearance, as they often struggle with a desire for beauty. It is lust to be consumed by how you look. There are some people, especially women, who always arrive late on occasions, no matter how important it is, because they are never easily satisfied with their appearances, and they spend an unreasonable amount of time trying to come out looking beautiful. There is also the lust to be famous, the lust for wealth and possessions, etc. Satan will present all these to you to make you slaves to them and to limit the impact of God's word in your life. Do not let him; you must flee all youthful lust.

♦ Idolatry

> "So, my dear friends, flee from the worship of idols." (1Cor. 10: 14 NLT)

God cannot tolerate another god in a believer's life. You should not allow anything else to become a god to you, no matter what it is, because God will judge it and destroy it. It is only when it concerns another god that the Bible says God becomes jealous (Exodus 34:14). Idolatry is placing anything above God or treating something as more precious and important than what you have with God.

To overcome idolatry, you must realise that we all have the tendency to make idols out of something that God has blessed us with, and we must be on the watch so that the things do not become idols to us. Decide not to fight, tooth and nail, for anything you like to have. Understand that you do not have to get everything you desire. Nonetheless, if you get to have what you desire, treat it as something to be used only, something that your life or happiness does not depend on and that you can do without.

You must have power over your possessions and not allow anything you possess to have power over you. You know that you have the power over your possessions when you can give them away easily and whenever you need to. The hoarding of things and an accumulative tendency are signs of idolatry. Do not be selfish with anything you have; you must learn to use it to bless other people. If you are becoming too attached to anything, give it away. Nothing must have power over you.

♦ Sexual sin

> "Run away from sexual sin! No other sin so clearly affects the body as this one does. For sexual immorality is a sin against your own body. [19] Or

92

> don't you know that your body is the temple of the
> Holy Spirit, who lives in you and was given to you
> by God? You do not belong to yourself, [20] for
> God bought you with a high price. So, you must
> honor God with your body" (1Cor. 6: 18- 20 NLT)

As a young person who desires to live for God, serve God, and stay out of trouble, you need to keep away from bad influences. Be selective about who your friends are and the places you go. Choose the things you watch on TV or the internet carefully. If you are single and do not want to sleep around, do not date an unbeliever. An unbeliever does not see anything wrong with having sex before marriage. If you are in a relationship or are dating a believer who keeps asking you for sex and it is not what you want to do until after marriage, you should be ready to end the relationship if he will not take a no for an answer. It is better to end a relationship and lose a friend than to lose the comfort of God's presence.

If you are married and you do not want to fall into extramarital relationships, avoid building unhealthy relationships with the opposite sex. To avoid an unhealthy relationship, here are four things to do:

(I)   Never spend more time with another man or woman (opposite sex) more time than you do with your spouse. You will inadvertently develop a deeper relationship and affection with the person with whom you spend the most time. People tend to care more about those who give them more attention.

(II)   Never make another man or woman (opposite sex) your best friend or close confidant besides your spouse. The chances of developing something special with someone who gives you attention and a caring hearing ear are extremely high. The person who you can pour your heart into and who will give you attention may end up becoming your confidant and could replace your spouse in your heart if it is another woman or man.

(III) End it and walk away when you sense that you are starting to enjoy the comfort and company of another man or woman (opposite sex) more than you enjoy your spouse's. If you do not end it and walk away, demons will have a chance to sow ideas into your head or the other person's head. It is always the case that when someone's feelings towards their spouse are waning, they will be growing on someone else, and it will be on the person whose company they enjoy the most.

(IV) Avoid giving a gift to another (opposite sex) that you cannot give or have never given to your spouse. The Bible says, "For where your treasure is there will your heart be also" (Matthew 6:21 KJV). You can tell where someone's heart is, by looking at where they are investing their treasures the most. It says a lot, and it should be concerning, if you are doing something for someone that you could not do and have never done for your spouse.

One way to know if you care more for someone else than you do for your spouse is to look at what you are doing for them.

CHAPTER 8

⌒◆⌒

BRINGING DEMONS
INTO SUBJECTION

Very importantly, to engage demons and bring them under subjection, you must first understand the following:

❖ Salvation is your highest value

Being saved is the most wonderful and powerful experience in anyone's life; it confers divine authority on the person. Anyone who is not born again remains subject to the Kingdom of Satan and under his authority; therefore, he cannot exercise any authority over demons.

It is foolish to seek to exercise authority over evil spirits; if you are not born again, they will mess you up as they did to certain people in Acts of the Apostle chapter 19, who were simply identified as the seven sons of Sceva. They did not have any experience of salvation; however, when they saw Paul cast out evil spirits, they tried to cast evil spirits as well, but they were instead overpowered and beaten by the evil spirits that were in the man that they sought to cast the evil spirits from, and they were left naked.

> "Seven sons of Sceva, a Jewish chief priest, were doing this. [15] One day the evil spirit answered them, "Jesus I know, and Paul I know about, but who are you?" [16] Then the man who had the evil spirit jumped on them and overpowered them all. He gave them such a beating that they ran out of the house naked and bleeding" (Acts 19:14-16 NIV).

The sons of Sceva lacked the authority to cast out evil spirits because they had no relationship with Jesus. Anyone who says he can drive out evil spirits but is not saved is lying, or he is being deceived.

Your salvation is superior to any gift, blessing, or position of authority that you may have. Salvation is the fundamental determining factor in how spirit beings will look at you or treat you. In the realm of the spirit, everything rises and falls with salvation, and if you are not saved, demons will play you like a football. Demons will only fear you, and submit to you, if your name is written in the book of life. In Luke Chapter 10, the disciples of Jesus went into towns and villages, preaching about the coming kingdom, and they came back with excitement because demons were subject to them in the name of Jesus. However, Jesus said to them:

> "…I saw Satan fall like lightning from heaven. [19] I have given you authority to trample on snakes

and scorpions and to overcome all the power of the enemy; nothing will harm you. [20] However, do not rejoice that the spirits submit to you, but rejoice that your names are written in heaven" (Luke 10:18-20 NIV).

In other words, Jesus was saying to them, it was wonderful that demons obeyed you in my name, and it is something for you to rejoice about. However, having demons obey you is not as important as having your names written in the book of life, and this is what is more important. Being born again places the believer in a position that is over and above demons.

❖ Your position in Christ Jesus is far above -

Satan became the god of this world and had authority to exercise dominion over the earth because, through the fall of Adam, he handed Satan the dominion God gave him over the earth. When Jesus died, He descended into hell, and in hell He defeated Satan and took back what Adam handed to him at the fall.

> "Forasmuch then as the children are partakers of flesh and blood, he also himself likewise took part of the same; that through death he might destroy him that had the power of death, that is, the devil; [15] And deliver them who through fear of death were all their lifetime subject to bondage" (Hebrews 2: 14-15 KJV).

Man's bondage to Satan ended because Jesus, through His death, paid in full the penalty of the sin, which gave Satan a legal hold over human being. In death, Jesus defeated Satan. He made a public spectacle of his demons and stripped them of their powers and the legal hold that they had over people.

> "Having canceled the charge of our legal indebtedness, which stood against us and condemned us; he has taken it away, nailing it to the cross. [15] And having disarmed the powers and authorities, he made a public spectacle of them, triumphing over them by the cross" (Colossians 2:14-15 NIV).

Because of what Jesus accomplished in death and resurrection, Satan lost all his powers that Adam handed to him. Satan no longer has dominion over the earth and can no longer determine the destiny of anybody who is saved and is a new creation in Christ Jesus. Jesus has declared that Satan has fallen (Luke 10:18-20 KJV). Therefore, the moment someone gives his life to Jesus, he becomes free from the power of darkness, he is immediately removed from satan's kingdom, and he is planted in the kingdom of Jesus, which is a position, higher and above the position Satan is. Demons are under the feet of anyone who belongs in the kingdom of Jesus (Ephesians 1: 15-23; Colossians 1:13-14).

To bring demons under subjection, you must understand your position in Christ Jesus and be aware of all the privileges that are available to you as a child of God. Satan will want you to think that he still has authority over you, and that he can do anything he likes with you, and can even determine your destiny, but that is only a lie of the devil. You are now a member of a superior kingdom; the kingdom of Jesus is superior, and Satan is under your feet. Therefore, you must be aware that:

- You are Delivered from the power of darkness and translated into the kingdom of Jesus (Colossians 1: 13).
- Satan's kingdom lost the authority over you and your destiny (Colossians 1: 13).
- You are Redeemed from curses; Satan cannot subject you to curses anymore (Galatians 3: 13).
- You are now Seated in the heavenly place in Christ, far above principalities and powers (Ephesians 2: 5-7).
- You are elevated to the highest place above demons (Ephesians 1: 20-23).
- You are now God's heir, and joint Heir with Christ. You now qualify to enjoy the goodness of God and walk in His blessings (Romans 8: 16-17).
- You are an ambassador for Christ here on earth; you carry heaven's mandate on you; you represent heaven wherever you go (2 Corinthians 5: 20).
- Angels are now your ministers; they are sent by God as your ministering spirits; they will carry out your assignments and protect you from all satanic attacks (Hebrews 1: 13-14).

One scriptural truth we must be clear about and established in is that Jesus stripped Satan of all powers when He died and went down into hell. Jesus disgraced Satan openly, triumphing over him when He rose from the dead. Now all powers in heaven and on earth belong to Jesus (Matthew 28:18).

Satan's ambition to be a god here on earth has not changed. He has not given up on his aspiration of being a god, and he seeks to be a god in the hearts of men and a god over communities, towns, cities, and nations. He still rules as a god in the lives of the people who are not saved, the people whose names are not written in heaven and who are still aligning themselves with him, in their philosophies and ideologies, and in the lifestyles they live. Satan can also exercise dominion in the lives of people who are living in ignorance or disobedience to God, whether they are saved or not. Always remember that ignorance and disobedience make a believer vulnerable. The Bible makes it clear that Satan will always have the advantage over the people who are living in ignorance (2 Corinthians 2:11).

❖ You have authority in Christ Jesus to cast out devils -

Jesus did not only take back the authority and dominion that Satan stole from Adam, but He also delegated it to believers when He said:

> "Behold, I give unto you power to tread on serpents and scorpions, and over all the power of the enemy: and nothing shall by any means hurt you" (Luke 10:19 KJV).

Every believer can now function under the delegated authority that is from Jesus, and with that authority, they can command, forbid, and cast out evil spirits. A believer does not have to be a pastor to be able to cast out demons; he has the authority to cast out demons, even if he only gave his life to Jesus yesterday.

> "And these signs will accompany those who believe: In my name they will drive out demons; they will speak in new tongues; [18] they will pick up snakes with their hands; and when they drink deadly

> poison, it will not hurt them at all; they will place
> their hands on sick people, and they will get well"
> (Mark 16:17-18 NIV).

The words of Jesus in the scripture above do not limit his authority to title men and women. The authority to lay hands on the sick and heal them, and the authority to cast out demons, belongs to every believer. The name of Jesus is believers' staff of authority, and Satan cannot deny it. Anytime a believer declares the name of Jesus, he reminds Satan of his defeat. Whenever a believer uses the name of Jesus, either to address spirits or for whatever reason, he brings to bear the power and dominance of Jesus's kingdom. When Jesus said to go in Matthew 28: 18-19, He was saying you are now His representative, wherever you are, and you will function under the power and authority of Jesus, and Satan can no longer dominate you. You must go about your life being conscious of this; do not allow the kingdom of darkness and their demon spirit to intimidate you.

❖ The place of Righteousness is your position of power -

> "In righteousness shalt thou be established: thou
> shalt be far from oppression; for thou shalt not fear:
> and from terror; for it shall not come near thee.
> [15] Behold, they shall surely gather together, but
> not by me: whosoever shall gather together against
> thee shall fall for thy sake. [17] No weapon that is
> formed against thee shall prosper; and every tongue
> that shall rise against thee in judgment thou shalt
> condemn. This is the heritage of the servants of the

LORD, and their righteousness is of me, saith the
LORD" (Isaiah 54:14-15,17 KJV)

A believer avails himself of the anointing of the Holy Spirit,
and he walks in power when he lives right with God. However,
he hinders the operation of the Holy Spirit in his life, and
the anointing will not be functional in his life when he lives
unrighteously, because the anointing, which symbolises the
power of God, flows only upon the person or in the place where
righteousness has become the norm. Living unrighteously is
equal to wickedness before God, and it stands in the way of
the anointing.

> "You have loved righteousness and hated
> wickedness; therefore God, your God, has set you
> above your companions by anointing you with the
> oil of joy" (Hebrews 1:9 NIV).

When someone loves righteousness, he will hate wickedness,
but if he embraces wickedness, he will live unrighteously and
do things that God considers wicked. A believer's position of
authority and power therefore is in the place of living right and
holy. Yes, faith in Christ Jesus confers the gift of righteousness
upon everyone who believes. Yes, God sees a believer as
someone who has not done anything wrong before because
of Jesus' redemption sacrifice. In Christ Jesus, the believer is
accepted by God unconditionally; he belongs in the kingdom
of Jesus, and he qualifies to enjoy the goodness of God. These
notwithstanding, a believer is required to walk in obedience to
God's word, to perfect holiness in the fear of God, and to avail
himself of what Jesus has provided.

> "Having therefore these promises, dearly beloved, let us cleanse ourselves from all filthiness of the flesh and spirit, perfecting holiness in the fear of God" (2 Corinthians 7:1 KJV).

The above scripture will be irrelevant if there is no connection whatsoever between the promises of God and believers needing to cleanse themselves from all filthiness of the flesh. The instruction is useless if the filthiness of the flesh cannot interfere with the promise of God. A believer cannot just claim the righteousness of God in Christ Jesus, only by word of mouth, and then go about living life contrary to the lifestyle that God requires believers to have and still enjoy the full benefits of his salvation. Living in obedience to God's word and in the fear of God is critical to someone enjoying the full benefits of salvation. The Bible says:

> "Son though he was, he learned obedience from what he suffered [9] and, once made perfect, he became the source of eternal salvation for all who obey him" (Hebrews 5:8-9 NIV).

Jesus being the source of eternal salvation means that it is Jesus who can bring about the fulfilment of all the benefits of salvation for any believer. The blessing of our redemption proceeds from him, and without his involvement, nothing happens. However, Jesus is only committed to making any believer enjoy the benefits of salvation if they walk in obedience to Him. Living contrary to God's word is a dangerous way for a believer; he forfeits a lot that Jesus can accomplish in him and through him. Living unrighteously shows contempt for God, and those who continue living in the uncleanliness of their ways are despising God, who called us to live holy.

> "For God hath not called us unto uncleanness,
> but unto holiness. [8] He therefore that despiseth,
> despiseth not man, but God, who hath also given
> unto us his Holy Spirit" (1 Thessalonians 4:7-8
> KJV).

Sin is Satan's invention; he makes the sin atmosphere his territory; he shows up wherever sin is prevalent; and anyone who submits to a lifestyle of sin comes under his authority. No one who subjects himself to living in a sinful territory can overpower demons; it is also one of the reasons why God says we should be holy. Anything God says to do is for our own good and not for God's benefit. There is nothing we do or do not do that will impact God; He is unchanging and the same yesterday, today, and forevermore.

Satan does not tempt believers and get them to sin just for the sake of it or to only offend God. No, Satan knows that the believer who submits to unrighteousness inadvertently submits to his authority. We make ourselves vulnerable to the enemy Satan, and we forfeit a lot anytime we live unrighteously, against the will and purpose of God.

> "Don't you know that when you offer yourselves
> to someone as obedient slaves, you are slaves of the
> one you obey-whether you are slaves to sin, which
> leads to death, or to obedience, which leads to
> righteousness?" (Romans 6:16 NIV)

Satan always has the upper hand against someone who is living in sin. No one who lives in sin and disregards the word of God and His demand for living a holy life will be able to fight off demon spirits. The implications of a sinful lifestyle also include the following:

A Sinful lifestyle weakens the believer's foundation

What forms a solid foundation in a believer's life is his hearing and doing what God's word says.

> "As for everyone who comes to me and hears my words and puts them into practice, I will show you what they are like. [48] They are like a man building a house, who dug down deep and laid the foundation on rock. When a flood came, the torrent struck that house but could not shake it, because it was well built. [49] But the one who hears my words and does not put them into practice is like a man who built a house on the ground without a foundation. The moment the torrent struck that house, it collapsed and its destruction was complete." (Luke 6:47-49 NIV).

The word of God puts a believer on a solid foundation. Therefore, if you keep obeying the Word, and doing whatever it says, no matter what Satan throws at you, you will win. The devil wants to get you to go against the Word living your life contrary to the Word, so he can weaken your foundation and win against you. You cannot do anything against Satan with a weakened foundation. The Bible says:

> "If the foundations be destroyed, what can the righteous do" (Psalm 11:3 KJV).

At some point in everyone's life, Satan will stir up the storm or bring adversity in some way. How firm they are going to stand during the storm or emerge after adversity will depend on how solid their foundation is. Satan causes adversity sometimes just to test the strength of your foundation, and he hopes that it will be a weak foundation. Never allow adversity to meet you when your foundation is weakened. And since you cannot tell when you will be thrust into stormy weather, ensure that your foundation stays strong by being a habitual doer of the word.

Sinful lifestyle creates a crack in the wall

Every believer has spiritual walls —the wall of defence. The walls keep demons out and keep believers safe and warm. When the walls of defence crack or fall, satanic arrows will penetrate through. The evil one shoots arrows at believers, and the arrows of evil may come in the form of sicknesses, diseases, arrows of death, arrows of financial ruin, arrows of miscarriage, arrows of business collapse, etc. A lot of believers are not aware that Satan likes to shoot arrows at them —all kinds of arrows. He always does, and as such, the Bible is saying to all believers:

> "In addition to all this, take up the shield of faith, with which you can extinguish all the flaming arrows of the evil one" (Ephesians 6:16 NIV).

A lot of damage happens to believers because of the evil arrows sent against them. When a believer ignores the word, his foundation starts to shake (Luke 6:47-49). And when the foundation starts to shake, the believer's safe habitat will be threatened, and the dweller will become vulnerable. This is because when the foundation starts to move, the wall of protection that is around the believer will also start to crack, and some things in his life will begin to go wrong because of those cracks.

> "Whoever digs a pit may fall into it; whoever breaks through a wall may be bitten by a snake" (Ecclesiastes 10:8 NIV).

There is a wall of protection around every believer, but it is the strength of the foundation they are standing on that keeps their wall intact. Satan is always going about, looking for an opportunity and someone to devour, and the opportunity he is looking for is a crack through which he can gain entry into someone's territory. The Bible warns believers:

> "Be alert and of sober mind. Your enemy the devil prowls around like a roaring lion looking for someone to devour" (1 Peter 5:8 NIV).

> "Leave no [such] room or foothold for the devil [give no opportunity to him]" (Ephesians 4:27 AMPC).

You must be aware that disobedience to God and living a sinful lifestyle are attacks against the foundation, and they create a crack in the wall of defence around the believer. That is the opportunity Satan is sprawling around looking for. You must make sure your foundation remains solid, in-tacked, and your wall fortified to keep the snakes away.

CHAPTER 9

CONTENDING WITH EVIL SPIRITS

By establishing yourself in the fundamental truth mentioned above, you position yourself in a place where Satan cannot bring you under his dominion. You must always remember that Satan is a liar. He uses lies and deception to thrive. Establish yourself in the truth of the revelation of the scriptures, and you will have an advantage over evil spirits. Understand that evil spirits do not operate physically here on earth because they do not have physical bodies, so they will have to enter human beings to operate. One of their deceptions is to make you see the people they have entered, taken control of, and are operating through as the enemy. However, the scriptures clearly show us that the battle we fight is not against people but againts spirits.

> "For our struggle is not against flesh and blood, but against the rulers, against the authorities, against the powers of this dark world and against the spiritual forces of evil in the heavenly realms." (Ephesians 6:12 NIV).

Demons may enter human beings or manipulate them from outside to harm us; however, we must not treat any human being who is being used by demons as an enemy and target them in our fight against evil, because it will be futile. The demons are simply going to move from one human being to another, in the demise of one, and will continue to fight against us. Always remember that your fight is against demon spirits and not human beings. Human beings, no matter who they are, are deserving of your love (Matthew 5:43-48).

Since your fight is against spirits and not people, you cannot make use of earthly weapons to contend with them; it will also be futile. The Bible clearly says that our weapons against spirits are not of this world:

> "The weapons we fight with are not the weapons of the world. On the contrary, they have divine power to demolish strongholds" (2 Corinthians 10:4 NIV).

I have seen all kinds of warfare prayers against evil spirits in believers' gatherings that I consider a total waste of the people's time because they contradict the scriptures. It is not possible to contend with evil spirits in a way that is not supported by the scriptures and prevail against them; it amounts to having no foundation to stand on. The spirit of error is that of Satan, and he is always going to use it to get believers to operate in error because he knows that they are not going to achieve any results while operating in error. Ignorance is no excuse; Satan is always going to capitalise on ignorance to thrive. For instance, warfare prayers such as the use of sticks and horsewhip to flog demons, the throwing of stones at evil spirits, the use of broom sticks to shoot arrows at demons, or the use of a hammer to break Satan's head are all useless prayers, and they don't do anything to spirits because believers' weapons of war are not of this world. Carnal weapons do nothing to spirit beings; they do not inflict any harm on them.

There are these other warfare prayers that do not also line up with scriptures and are therefore ineffective, which you must be aware of. You must understand that you cannot pray to send Satan or demons to hell or to the bottomless pit. They still have time to roam this earth and will continue to do so freely until the end of time appointed for them. Demons will move freely upon the earth, and you cannot send demons to hell because their appointed time has been fixed (Matthew 8:29; Revelation 20:1-3). Furthermore, you cannot bind the devil or demons in the sense that you are chaining them or handcuffing them so that they cannot move about. Many believers use Matthew 16, where Jesus said, "I will give you the keys of the kingdom of heaven; whatever you bind on earth will be bound in heaven, and whatever you loose on earth will be loosed in heaven" ("Matthew 16:19 NIV), as the supporting scripture for binding the demons, as in chaining them, or tying them down, and forbidden them from movement.

The binding and losing in this context are not particularly referring to dealing with demons. It is referring to believers' authority to permit something here on earth or to disallow it. And whatever they permit or disallow, heaven will sanction it. Jesus makes the same declaration further down, in the 18th chapter of Matthew and verse 18, and he makes it clearer there. Jesus discusses the power and authority of believers to make decisions that they agree upon, which will be endorsed in heaven. In other words, Jesus is saying that any decision that the church shall take on any matter here on earth will be upheld in heaven, as the position of the church and heaven will enforce it.

The crucial point of Jesus's statement in Matthew 18 is related to the relationship among believers. One of the authorities Jesus has vested in the church is the ability to resolve conflicts. The composition of the church places every believer accountable to the church. Being a part of the church puts every believer in a position where he can be taught, guided, instructed, corrected, and even rebuked. This helps to keep every believer on the right track. God ordained the church assembly so that believers can be constantly guided theologically and doctrinally and to be instructed in righteousness. That way, they are protected from error and satanic influences (Acts 2:42 KJV). The church also has the authority to judge and settle disputes among believers.

> "Do ye not know that the saints shall judge the world? and if the world shall be judged by you, are ye unworthy to judge the smallest matters? [3] Know ye not that we shall judge angels? How much more things that pertain to this life? [4] If then ye have judgments of things pertaining to this life, set them to judge who are least esteemed in the church. [5] I speak to your shame. Is it so, that there is not a wise man among you? no, not one that shall be able to judge between his brethren?" (1 Corinthians 6:2-5 KJV).

This authority vested in the church makes it significantly important for the church to be the pillar and ground of truth and to uphold the truth and godly principles when dealing with all matters, especially in judging issues among brethren.

> "But if I tarry long, that thou mayest know how thou oughtest to behave thyself in the house of God, which is the church of the living God, the pillar and ground of the truth" (1 Timothy 3:15 KJV).

Therefore, believers are required to bring their unresolved disputes to the church, and the church is to serve as the final arbiter of fairness and justice in all matters. And the church must be the pillar and ground of truth in all matters. The church is the final arbiter of justice for believers because it is the body of Jesus, His physical representation here on earth, and therefore speaks on behalf of Jesus. Whatever the church allows or disallows, heaven will enforce it. And Jesus says that anyone who refuses the justice of the church should be regarded as a pagan, as someone who is the same as an infidel and idol worshipper.

> "If your brother or sister sins, go and point out their fault, just between the two of you. If they listen to you, you have won them over. [16] But if they will not listen, take one or two others along, so that 'every matter may be established by the testimony of two or three witnesses.' [17] If they still refuse to listen, tell it to the church; and if they refuse to listen even to the church, treat them as you would a pagan or a tax collector. [18] "Truly I tell you, whatever you bind on earth will be bound in heaven, and whatever you loose on earth will be loosed in heaven" (Matthew 18:15-18 NIV).

The binding and losing Jesus speaks of is not about chaining demons. You cannot bind demons. However, you can forbid them from operating in a domain where you have rights, like your own affairs, your home, your family, your church, etc. Though you can forbid demons from operating in your own affairs. However, you cannot chain or forbid demons from operating in your town, city, or nation. It is important to know that you can only forbid demons from operating in your domain, or the territory that you have influence over. You cannot also pray to kill the demons, because they are spirit beings, so the 'fall down and die" declaration is useless; it does not do anything to demons; spirits do not fall and die; they are eternal beings, and a lake of fire awaits them at the end of times. You must understand that, for any prayer to be effective, it must line up with scripture. Your prayers are accompanied by the power of the Holy Spirit only when they are in line with God's Word.

Exercising your authority over evil spirits

Here are a few things you can do to exercise your authority over demon spirits:

❖ Bring all ungodly and negative thoughts into captivity

> "For the weapons of our warfare are not carnal, but mighty through God to the pulling down of strong holds; 5 Casting down imaginations, and every high thing that exalteth itself against the knowledge of God and bringing into captivity

every thought to the obedience of Christ"
(2 Corinthians 10:4-5 KJV).

I said earlier that Satan's first battle ground is the thought realm. He knows that if he can gain control over someone's mind and thinking pattern, he will be able to control his life and behaviour. Therefore, Satan will do everything possible to take control of people's thoughts. And he has assigned his power demons to bombard human minds and seek to control them. To have control over someone's mind and thoughts, Satan would plant his ideology, human wisdom and philosophy, and all kinds of ungodly imaginations. He understands that the scripture says, "For as he thinketh in his heart, so is he...." (Proverbs 23: 7 KJV). Whoever wins the battle of the mind will have the power of control. We must therefore engage in the mental battle against Satan, and we must overcome there to bring him to submission.

Satan succeeded in holding captive the people of Noah's generation, and he ruined them because he succeeded in holding their thoughts captive. God destroyed the people of that generation, not necessarily because of their evil ways but because their minds were completely taken over by demons, and God saw that their thoughts and imaginations were set on doing evil continually. Because Satan held their minds under siege, they were destined to never change.

> "And God saw that the wickedness of man was great in the earth, and that every imagination of the thoughts of his heart was only evil continually. [6] And it repented the LORD that he had made man on the earth, and it grieved him at his heart. [7] And the LORD said, I will destroy man whom

> I have created from the face of the earth; both man,
> and beast, and the creeping thing, and the fowls of
> the air; for it repenteth me that I have made them"
> (Genesis 6: 5-7 KJV).

Your thought life is the manufacturer of your behaviour and, consequently, is the determinant of the outcome of your life. In the battle of the mind against Satan, you must make sure you overcome evil, ungodly, and negative thoughts and not accept whatever Satan is flooding your mind with. If you can defeat Satan in the mind battle, you will have power over his schemes, and he cannot stop you. Satan will not and cannot exercise any control over you until and unless he first conquers you in the mind battles. Satan is never going to stop bombarding you with all kinds of evil thoughts and imaginations; he hopes to win someday. He will attack you from all directions. But you must learn to do a few things to keep your mind pure and to be in a place where you can hear God and be in tune with Him. The following are things you can do to maintain control over your thoughts:

♦ Sieve the things you watch and listen

You must learn to sieve what your mind takes in. It is not everything that you are going to allow your mind to absorb. The Bible says:

> "The light of the body is the eye: if therefore thine
> eye be single, thy whole body shall be full of light"
> (Mathew 6: 22 KJV).

You control what your mind takes in by controlling what you feed your eyes with and what you give your ears to. The eyes and ears are gateways to the mind. What you hear or behold is transmitted to your mind. And your mind is always going to play back what you see or hear in thought form. And the things that you play back in your mind may settle in your mind and develop into desires or cravings, which may influence your action. The things you watch and what you are listening to can enter your mind and dominate it. Gossip can affect your attitude towards somebody if you hear and allow it. If you entertain a negative comment about you and meditate over it, it may settle inside you and attack your confidence. If you are listening to words that contradict scripture, your faith will not grow.

Never think that the words you constantly hear and the things you are feeding your eyes with do not matter and will have no effect on you. It will only be a matter of time before they shape how you are thinking and, consequently, how you are behaving. This is why Jesus said, the light of the body is the eye. What you feed your eyes with is going to eventually have an influence on shaping the direction of your life.

♦ Constantly engage in the renewing of your mind

To have power over your mind, you must constantly engage in renewing it, as the Bible says.

> "And be not conformed to this world: but be ye transformed by the renewing of your mind, that ye may prove what is that good, and acceptable, and perfect, will of God" (Romans 12:2 KJV).

Mind-renewal means you are consciously exercising your mind to bring your thoughts, feelings, and emotions in line with the word of God. Mind-renewal is the process through which you flush out from your mind all thoughts, ideas, reasoning, feelings, and emotions that are not in consonance with the word of God, and allowing the word of God to fill your mind and form the basis of your reasoning and judgement.

Sometimes Satan subtly gets in your mind, and he plants negative thoughts and ideas. He takes advantage of the trying seasons in your life, or the rough situations you are going through, to attack you in your thought life. He may use those occasions to sow the seeds of revenge or the seeds of harming people who have offended or hurt you, especially if it was an offence that you were dealing with. He will sow self-dejection or suicidal thoughts when you are going through failure or experiencing disappointment. He will sow immoral thoughts when you are alone or with someone who creates the opportunity for you to feel that way. He will use human reasoning to influence how you perceive things. You will need to constantly renew your mind because you are constantly going to be bombarded by demons. You can renew your mind by redirecting your thoughts to what the word of God says about your situation. Go to the Word of God daily and meditate on the scriptures that speak about your situation. Use those scriptures and speak aloud to yourself. You need to hear yourself speak those words aloud.

One of Satan's reasons for bombarding your mind is to get you to develop a thought pattern that is not in alignment with the word of God. He is fully aware that, until your mindset lines up with what God's word says, you are not going to be able to know what the good, acceptable, and perfect will of God is (Roman 12:2). He knows that you cannot differentiate between Satan's idea and God's idea until your mind is renewed. There are many people floating demon ideas as God's idea, and they are genuinely convinced it is God's idea. However, they are wrong; their minds have been corrupted by demons, and their thoughts are influenced by demons. No matter how good something appears or sounds, it cannot be God's idea if it does not agree with the word of God.

♦ Attack every demonic whisper

Demons will constantly try to violate your thoughts and influence how you think. They are going to try to infiltrate it and plant negative thoughts and evil imaginations. Occasionally, particularly in your difficult and challenging moments, demons will whisper to you to do something stupid. Your mind may be flooded with all kinds of thoughts, and they will be so loud as to drown out the still small voice coming from your heart.

The difference between demonic whispers and the voice of your spirit is that the demon's whispers will be in your head, while your spirit will speak to you from your heart. You must always rebuke the whispers of demons and not give them an inch of space in your mind. Do not think about them, do not meditate over them, and rebuke those thoughts in your head that do not line up with your heart conviction.

> "Finally, brothers and sisters, whatever is true, whatever is noble, whatever is right, whatever is pure, whatever is lovely, whatever is admirable-if

anything is excellent or praiseworthy-think about
such things" (Philippians 4:8 NIV).

Always follow your heart and not your head when you feel
bombarded by different thoughts. When you hear thoughts
like you are a failure, a big fool, go kill yourself; there is nothing
wrong with it; she is your enemy, fight back; it doesn't matter;
no one sees you; no one will know; everybody is doing it; you
don't have to return it to them; you can't allow her to talk to
you that way; don't be a fool; give it back to them in the same
coin, etc. In those circumstances, speak to those demons and
rebuke them. Always remember that you sometimes need to
hear yourself speak God's word aloud. Demons do not know
what you are thinking until you act. In the same vein, you
cannot rebuke demons in your mind; you must speak aloud.

You are more prone to demonic whispers in difficult and
challenging times. In those times, learn to occupy your mind
with the Word and speak it aloud to yourself. Speak to the
situation according to what the word of God says. Do not
give room to demons to speak to you (Romans 10: 8-10; 2
Corinthians 4: 13). For instance, when things are hard for you,
declare Philippians 4: 13 over you. When you are experiencing
lack, declare Philippians 4: 19 over you. When you feel you
are being attacked by fear, speak aloud, "God hath not given
us the spirit of fear; but of power, and love, and a sound mind
(2 Timothy 1: 7 KJV). When you feel weak and powerless,
declare to yourself, "The Lord is my light and my salvation;
whom shall I fear? The Lord is the strength of my life; of whom
shall I be afraid? When the wicked, even my enemies and my
foes, came upon me to eat up my flesh, they stumbled and fell.
Though an enemy should encamp against me, my heart shall

not fear; though war should rise against me, in this will I be confident" (Psalms 27: 1-3 KJV). Do not accept the situation you are in, do not agree with Satan's suggestion, and do not declare to yourself whatever he says to you. He is a liar.

Gossips are demon whispers. Do not entertain gossip; it pollutes your mind against the people you love and care about, and it can ruin relationships. When anyone is trying to gossip about somebody to you, learn to tell them politely but firmly that you do not like gossip. You do not want to change the impression you have about the person in question because you care about them. When someone offends you, forgive them very quickly, even before they realise that they offended you; do not let the sun go down on your anger (Ephesians 6: 26-27). If you do not forgive as quickly as it happens, the devil can take advantage of the situation and plant in your mind all sorts of negative ideas about the person. You must do everything possible to protect your mind so that nothing contrary gets the chance to settle in it.

❖ Take a stand

> "Therefore, take up the whole armor of God, that you may be able to withstand in the evil day, and having done all, to stand" (Ephesians 6:13 NKJV).

You must take a stand against Satan to bring him into subjection, and you have authority in the name of Jesus to do so. You must never back down from Satan. Satan and his demons have tenacity; they are not going to walk away easily until they can see that you know your covenant place in Christ Jesus. When you stand on the authority of the Word of God and in the name of Jesus and say no to Satan over a particular situation, he has no choice but to flee.

> "Submit yourselves therefore to God. Resist the devil, and he will flee from you" (James 4:7 KJV).

You stand your ground when you refuse to yield to temptation. You stand your ground when you refuse to accept the contrary, and you insist on what the word of God says, irrespective of what you are seeing or hearing. And there are times you will have to speak out and tell the devil, instructing him to back down in the name of Jesus. A good example here is the temptation experienced by Jesus in Matthew 4: 1-11. We saw that Satan was having a counter-exchange of scriptures with Jesus, and it did not deter Satan that Jesus knew the scripture and could quote it. Satan has tenacity; he will persist for as long as you give him an audience. We saw that Satan left and departed from Jesus only after He commanded, "Get out of here, Satan."

> "Then Jesus was led by the Spirit into the wilderness to be tempted there by the devil. [2] For forty days and forty nights he fasted and became very hungry. [3] During that time the devil came and said to him, if you are the Son of God, tell these stones to become loaves of bread. [4] But Jesus told him, No! The Scriptures say, 'People do not live by bread alone, but by every word that comes from the mouth of God. [5] Then the devil took him to the holy city, Jerusalem, to the highest point of the Temple, [6] and said, "If you are the Son of God, jump off! For the Scriptures say, 'He will order his angels to protect you. And they will hold you up

with their hands, so you won't even hurt your foot on a stone. [7] Jesus responded, "The Scriptures also say, 'You must not test the Lord your God. [8] Next the devil took him to the peak of a very high mountain and showed him all the kingdoms of the world and their glory. [9] I will give it all to you," he said, "if you will kneel down and worship me. [10] Get out of here, Satan, Jesus told him. "For the Scriptures say, you must worship the Lord your God and serve only him. [11] Then the devil went away, and angels came and took care of Jesus" (Matthew 4:1-11 NLT).

If you give the devil the chance, he is going to argue with you, even over the scripture, and for as long as it takes; he has all the time. He will leave you alone, but only if you command him to leave. Jesus knew that too. Everything Jesus did, he did it to leave us an example so that we could follow in His steps. You must know when to give demons firm and clear instructions. It is good to declare scripture over the situation or speak it over you; however, in taking a stand against Satan, you must know when to command him in the name of Jesus. Learn to use words such as Get behind me, Satan. Leave now, in Jesus' name. I rebuke you; you go now. I reject that; it is not my portion. Receive healing in the name of Jesus. I cast you out; go now, you foul spirit, etc. Note that you cannot bind Satan, and you cannot send Satan to hell, as I explained above. You must be authoritative when you are dealing with demons. The way you talk to God should be different from the way you talk to demons. When talking to God, you are to plead your case and show humility. But not so with demons. You do not plead with demons; you are to command them authoritatively in the name of Jesus.

You release the full force of heaven anytime you speak authoritatively in the name of Jesus. The name of Jesus is the highest name above all names, whether they be in heaven or on earth, and demons cannot deny that name.

> "Wherefore God also hath highly exalted him, and given him a name which is above every name: [10] That at the name of Jesus every knee should bow, of things in heaven, and things in earth, and things under the earth; [11] And that every tongue should confess that Jesus Christ is Lord, to the glory of God the Father" (Philippians 2: 9-11 KJV).

The name of Jesus is given to us for defense and covering against attacks from any enemy (Psalm 20:1-2; Proverbs 18: 10). In warfare against evil spirits, the name of Jesus represents the believer's staff of office or the symbol of his authority. There is nothing in any human being that scares the devil; it is Jesus inside of believers that makes the difference (2 Corinthians 3:4-5). When Jesus said we can use his name, he meant that any time his name is used, He will act as though He were the one speaking to enforce it.

❖ Obedience to the Holy Spirit

> "And having in a readiness to revenge all disobedience, when your" obedience is fulfilled" (2 Corinthians 10:6 KJV).

I have explained earlier the importance of walking in obedience to God. You must never forget that you are only ready and equipped to bring evil spirits into subjection when you are walking in obedience to the leading of the Holy Spirit in your life. Outside of the leadership of the Holy Spirit, you are on your own, vulnerable, and powerless. You must also understand that there is nothing you can do to compensate for obedience. Your obedience to God means more than anything you can offer Him in sacrifice.

> "And Samuel said, Hath the Lord as great delight in burnt offerings and sacrifices, as in obeying the voice of the Lord? Behold, to obey is better than sacrifice, and to hearken than the fat of rams" (1 Samuel 15:22 KJV).

You cannot replace obedience with acts of kindness, with tithes, offerings, seeds of faith, first fruits, or anything else. If you ignore what you know God wants you to do, no amount of offering and tithes can substitute for it. Anytime you are walking in obedience to God, you become more than a conqueror; the enemy cannot succeed against you. He may flood your domain with all kinds of storms; however, you are going to withstand them (Luke 6: 47-49).

To exercise your authority over evil spirits, you must commit to two levels of obedience. Firstly, you must order your life and affairs according to the teaching of God's word. The word of God must be your watch and guiding principles in all you do, and you are not to allow the world principle and the pressure of life to shape your values or lifestyle. Secondly, you must commit to following the specific instructions or the leading of God for you. Jesus, with the help of the Holy Spirit, wants to guide you and show you what to do daily. He says:

"....... I am the Lord thy God which teacheth thee
to profit, which leadeth thee by the way that thou
shouldest go" (Isaiah 48:17 KJV).

When you follow God through the leading of the Holy Spirit, you will not fail, because God will not lead you to where you are not going to be victorious. Satan may fight against you, but God will have your back because He says He will teach you to profit and lead you in the direction that you should go. You can only fail when you ignore or set aside His authority over your life.

Your guarantee of victory over the demon's attack is linked to your knowing what God is saying for you to do and your obedience to Him. Never ignore God's leading in your life. Disobeying spiritual instruction will result in defeat by evil spirits. Understand that your prayer and fasting will not change anything because they are ineffective as long as you are ignoring what God is saying to you. Walking in obedience is a powerful weapon that the believer has against evil spirits. You must never base your actions on your own human wisdom and understanding of things, because they are limited. There are lots of things happening around us, and in the spirit, that you do not know of. There are evil forces all around you that you cannot see except God opens your eyes, and they are always orchestrating something against you that you have no clue about. You do not know what is coming your way; only God sees everything and can tell the future from the beginning (Isaiah 46:9-10). Left to your human understanding, you will always make a mistake and get many things wrong. The Bible says:

"There is a way that seemeth right unto a man, but the end thereof are the ways of death" (proverbs 14:12 KJV).

Human wisdom is sometimes foolishness (1 Corinthians 3:17), it has its limits. What seems right to you may be what Satan is waiting for you to do so he can break you to pieces. You cannot fight spirits with human wisdom or natural weapons. You must rely on the Holy Spirit. The scripture admonishes you to not lean on your own understanding but to trust the Lord to direct your paths (Proverbs 3:5-7 KJV). I admonish you to develop a high sensitivity to the Holy Spirit, understand His leading in your life, always do whatever He says, and go wherever He leads you, even when it makes no sense to you or appears foolish. Under the leadership of the Holy Spirit, you are powerful; you are more than a conqueror, and Satan and his demons will never win against you. Believers are powerless; they fail, suffer defeat, and come into harm when they do not listen to the voice of the Holy Spirit.

CHAPTER 10

❧◆❧

THE POWER OF DOING GOOD

"Do not be overcome by evil but overcome evil with good" (Romans 12:21 NIV).

The way to combat evil and evil spirits is completely different from how to deal with human beings, who are being influenced and manipulated by evil spirits. God left believers in this world and did not take them straight to heaven after their conversion because he needed them here on earth to show forth His glory and to help evangelize the rest of the people. Believers must therefore be mindful of this fact and be ready to show forth God's glory, wherever they are and through all their experiences.

It is also important for believers to go about being conscious that, though they are in the world they are not of this world. Hence, their view of the world, and people around them, their own lifestyles, and their approach to handling situations must be different from the rest of the people (Romans 12:1-3). The believer's power and authority over the world's system, and the spirits behind the world's system, are in the manifestation of their differences from the rest of the people. As believers display their differences, they are showing forth their sonship to God (Romans 8:19), and that is where their power over the world system lies. Believers' power and the authority Jesus vested in the church become impotent when believers' views of the world, the way they go about their lives, and their handling of their affairs are the same as how the rest of the people work.

The power vested in the believer is potent, effective, and life-transforming, only when they are living life differently and within the principles of God's Word. However, as believers choose to live differently from the rest of the people, they will attract persecution. Anytime believers seek to demonstrate their difference in their own domain and live as Jesus would, Satan stirs up trouble for them to stop them. Jesus says,

> "If ye were of the world, the world would love his own: but because ye are not of the world, but I have chosen you out of the world, therefore the world hateth you. [20] Remember the word that I said unto you, the servant is not greater than his lord. If they have persecuted me, they will also persecute you; if they have kept my saying, they will keep yours also" (John 15: 19-20 KJV).

The kingdom of Satan gets provoked, and it is threatened, when believers live by their separate set of rules upholding God's kingdom rules and showing forth His glory. Satan will always try to stop believers from living their lives differently. He knows that believers light will be dimmed, their authority will be diminished, and their influence in the world will be limited if they are living in a way that is the same as everyone. In order to stop believers, Satan will always stir up persecution against them. Understand that this is why people who don't love God, who are angry with the teachings of the scripture, who have no regard for Christian values, detest your lifestyle, hate you, seek to harm you, call you homophobic, and desire for you to be ostracized from your community.

You will be tagged as old-fashioned, antisocial, bigot, and a lawbreaker. You will be prejudiced against; some believers will lose their jobs; some will get expelled from schools and the clubs they go to. Some will be put in prison, while others will be put to death, all because of the values believers hold. However, amid all these, as a believer, you must choose to live differently from the people of the world, no matter the cost to you. Satan will do everything possible to get believers to conform to this world's system. Satan is comfortable when believers compromise their values; then the light of the gospel will not shine bright. Moreover, Satan's kingdom grows and establishes itself in all spheres of human experience when believers shell-in and do not live out who they are in Christ Jesus.

In talking about believers living by a different set of rules, a fundamental difference between believers in Christ and the rest of the people is the scriptural teachings, which believers must uphold. And that is to not pay back evil for evil, harm for harm, or hurt for hurt. The forces believers contend with are not human beings, but the forces of darkness that are operating in this world.

> "For our struggle is not against flesh and blood, but against the rulers, against the authorities, against the powers of this dark world and against

the spiritual forces of evil in the heavenly realms"
(Ephesians 6:12 NIV)

The forces of darkness are the ones who inhabit human beings, and they use them to persecute and afflict believers. You must not shift your focus from evil spirits in your good fight of faith and engage in a fight with human beings. Do not forget that one of Satan's strategies is to make you see people as your enemies, so you will engage them in a futile fight. Satan does not want believers to have cordial relationships, either among themselves or with the rest of the people, because he knows about the power of believers' agreement, and the impact of believers influence in a peaceful coexistence with others. He knows that believers will become unstoppable if they agree with each other. And he does not want believers to have cordial relationships with the rest of the people, because he knows that believers' peaceful coexistence with everyone will not only enable them to thrive in this world but will also make them effective representatives of Jesus in their community and will make many come to the saving knowledge about Jesus. The reason, therefore, for believers to insist on following peace with all men (Mark 9:50; Romans 12:18; Hebrews 12:14), is so that they can be effective ambassadors for Christ, wherever they are located.

Satan stirs up hatred against believers to curtail their reach and diminish the potency of the power of the gospel. He knows that where a believer is not received, their witness to Jesus will be missed. Without any effective Christian witness in any community, darkness will thrive there, and the people in the community will remain in Satan's bondage. It is critical, therefore, that, as a believer, whenever you are persecuted, you go past the people and see Satan behind it.

Do not forget that Satan is not only after the relationship between believers and those who do not believe; he seeks to ruin the relationship among believers as well, because he also knows that believers need each other to get to their destiny, and he wants to separate them, so they do not find the help that they need. Satan also knows that the word of God says to follow peace with all men and holiness, without which no man shall see God (Hebrews 12:14); he knows the scripture and understands that as long as believers are in contention and having rancor with one another, they will not see God move in their midst, and they will not see the power of the Holy Spirit working to bring transformation, and the revival the church is praying for will not come.

There is evil taking place all over the place, and there are people that evil spirits are influencing to cause people harm. However, there is no evil deployed by Satan that a believer lacks the power to contend with, and it does not matter which way it comes or through whom it comes. You will encounter evil people at your workplace, in your neighborhood, in your schools, and on the streets, and wherever you go, they are positioned by Satan to ruin God's purpose here on earth. They attack people to ruin what God is seeking to do through the people on earth. God wants you to live in victory over every evil design. With God's help, you can conquer every evil that confronts you. However, you must come to terms with what God said; you can only overcome evil with good.

"Do not be overcome by evil but overcome evil with good" (Romans 12:21 NKJV).

Romans 12:21 makes it clear that the believer cannot overcome darkness with darkness, quench fire with fire, subdue anger with anger, or defeat evil with evil. To exercise authority over evil and to defeat it, the believer will have to counter it with good, operating with heaven's system and not with the world's system. Heaven's system of operation may look foolish, but it is the wisdom of God. The following are the scriptural ways of dealing with all people in all situations:

❖ To walk in love with all men

"Ye have heard that it hath been said, thou shalt love thy neighbor, and hate thine enemy. [44] But I say unto you, Love your enemies, bless them that curse you, do good to them that hate you, and pray for them which despitefully use you, and persecute you; [45] That ye may be the children of your Father which is in heaven: for he maketh his sun to rise on the evil and on the good, and sendeth rain on the just and on the unjust" (Matthew 5: 43-45 KJV).

Believers are called to love both their neighbor and their enemy, as stated in the Bible verses above. A believer has the capacity to love and to love people authentically because, in the new birth, the love of God is shed abroad in their hearts by the Holy Spirit (Roman 5:5). For a believer, it is never the question of whether they have the capacity to love or not. Believers have the capacity to love. It is the question of whether they will choose to love or refuse to love. Believers must choose to walk in love with all people, irrespective of their background, color, race, gender, religious affiliation, or sexuality. Believers are not instructed to only love other believers but to love all human beings. And they are not to treat any human being as an enemy, no matter what they do to them.

Know that people are going to hate you, but you cannot hate them back. There must never be a room for hate in your heart. People may see you as their enemy and treat you badly, but you are to love them still, treat them with love, and extend to them God's mercy. If the Devil can get you to hate someone, he will defeat you. If the people that you have no love for attack you, they are going to succeed because you are not covered and have no love for them in your heart. You can only overcome evil with good.

❖ Follow the path of peace

People who do not like you, do not want to see you, and wish you would disappear will confront you. They will sometimes do things deliberately to offend you. The Bible instructs you to follow the way of peace when confronted by evil.

> "Do not repay anyone evil for evil. Be careful to do what is right in the eyes of everyone. [18] If it is possible, as far as it depends on you, live at peace with everyone" (Romans 12:17-18 NIV).

It must be observed that wherever there is no peace between you and someone, it is because they are not dependent on you. It must be seen that you went all the way and have done everything possible, but it is the other person who is rejecting your offer of peace. It must never be that there are disputes between you and someone, and you are the difficult party to deal with. You cannot defeat evil by being an unpeaceful person. A child of God must be a seeker of peace and a peacemaker.

> "Blessed (enjoying enviable happiness, spiritually prosperous-with life-joy and satisfaction in God's favour and salvation, regardless of their outward conditions) are the makers and maintainers of peace, for they shall be called the sons of God!" (Matthew 5:9 AMPC).

Satan never wins against peacemakers. They are operating in the class of God, the sons of God. Hatred and strife never win against peace. If you stick to the way of peace, regardless, favor and joy will pursue you. Seeking peace with all men and pursuing it may seem to other people as a sign of weakness, but that is not correct; it is a sign of strength. It takes a lot of strength and courage to ignore offense and reach out with a hand of friendship, returning peace for hurt and good for evil. The scripture says that anyone who loves life and desires to see good days must seek peace and pursue it. Those who want to live long should chase after peace.

> "For he that will love life, and see good days, let him refrain his tongue from evil, and his lips that they speak no guile: [11] Let him eschew evil, and do good; let him seek peace, and ensue it" (1 Peter 3:10-11 KJV).

In following the way of peace, learn to forgive quickly when you are offended; do not let the sun go down on your anger

(Ephesians 4:26), in other words, keep shining your light even when you are offended. When you get angry for whatever reason, you must still be in control of your emotions, watch your actions, and not act irrationally or contrary to God's word (Ephesians 4:26). Remember, you are a child of Christ. Bring your anger under control as quickly as possible, because in anger you cannot get things right before God (James 1:20). Anger gives the devil a foothold (Ephesians 4:27). Learn to choose your words carefully; do not act or speak out of rashness, anger, or a sense of injustice. Always make sure you are calm, in control, and under God's influence in your speaking.

Those who seek peace and pursue it are careful with their use of words. How you speak to people can either calm things down or aggravate them. How something is worded is vitally important; it can breed conflict or minister grace and peace. Many people do not know how to talk; they say anything as it comes to their mind, not realizing that there are demon spirits locking around seeking opportunities to whisper to them. They tell them, just say your mind, and they repeat it aloud, "I am just going to speak my mind and will say it as it sounds." Do not always say your mind, except you are operating with a transformed mind, according to Romans 12:1-3. What is in your mind may have been put there by the devil; you do not have to accept it, and you should not give it strength by giving it a voice.

A believer must constantly watch what occupies his mind and where its source is from, and he must always watch how he talks, because what he says can determine a lot in his relationships. Watch the following scriptures:

★ "A soft answer turneth away wrath: but grievous words stir up anger" (Proverbs 15:1 KJV).

★ "There is one who speaks like the piercings of a sword, but the tongue of the Wise promotes health" (Proverbs 12:18 NKJV).

★ "Let your speech be always with grace, seasoned with salt, that ye may know how ye ought to answer every man" (Colossians 4:5-6 KJV).

Satan, our enemy, is the primary cause of the problems we have with people, and because of that, we need to always look beyond the people or situation and see the spiritual forces that are taking advantage of the people's weaknesses and the situation. Do not fight with people when you are meant to be fighting with demon spirits. The people you are fighting may have been positioned by God as your helpers of destiny, and you could be their helpers of destiny too, but Satan is creating the problem you are having with them so he could stand on the way of your destiny or their destiny.

❖ Act in the opposite way

You often hear people say, when speaking of forgiveness, 'I have forgiven them, but I will not forget it, or they will say, 'I forgave them, but I will need to be careful with how I relate to them.' That is not God's kind of forgiveness. The kind of forgiveness that God asked us to give is the kind of forgiveness He showed us in Christ.

> "Be kind and compassionate to one another, forgiving each other, just as in Christ God forgave you" (Ephesians 4:32 NIV).

Forgiveness is not a Biblical forgiveness and is not acceptable to God until it is given in the manner which God forgave us. Here are some important things about God's forgiveness:

- ◆ He forgave us all.
- ◆ He blotted all offenses out of the record.
- ◆ He chose not to remember them anymore.
- ◆ He looks at us as though we have never offended him.
- ◆ He drew us closer to him.
- ◆ And He replaced our curse with His blessings.

  (Colossians 1:21-22; Colossians 2:13-14; Isaiah 43:24; Jeremiah 31:34; Hebrews 10:17)

When you give someone God's kind of forgiveness, you give them a clean slate, you hold nothing against them, you remove every inhibition standing in the way of you enjoying your relationship with them, and you bless them. When you are walking in forgiveness, you show people mercy and kindness.

God's kind of forgiveness empowers someone to not pay people back with their own coins. God's kind of forgiveness generates in the person who gives it the capacity to act towards the other person in the "opposite spirit," such that he can bless when insulted and cursed. He returns love for hatred. He prays for his persecutors in compliance with the scripture, which says:

> "Repay no one evil for evil. Have regard for good things in the sight of all men. If it is possible, as

much as depends on you, live peaceably with all men. Beloved, do not avenge yourselves, but rather give place to wrath; for it is written, Vengeance is Mine, I will repay, says the Lord. Therefore, if your enemy is hungry, feed him; if he is thirsty, give him a drink; for in so doing you will heap coals of fire on his head. Do not be overcome by evil, but overcome evil with good" (Romans 12:17-21 NKJV).

You go ahead today and make that phone call. Let the person at the other end of the phone hear you say, 'I forgive you from my heart.' It does not matter what they did to you; let it go completely. Now, reach out and send them the support you withheld. Share with them the information you have that can help them move forward, which you withheld because you were upset with them. Feed your enemies, give them drink, and let your good over their evil.

ACKNOWLEDGEMENTS

To the King eternal, immortal, invisible, and the only wise God, be all the glory and praise for giving me the inspiration for this book. I am grateful to my beautiful and adorable wife, Pastor Eunice Meque Bako, and my lovely children, Dorcas Rheece, Melissa Rangmen, and Jethro Men, for their continuing support and patience with my unavailability while authoring this book. I am profoundly grateful to God for the privilege of being the senior pastor of the RCCG Victory Assembly family for 23 years. Thank you, VA, for partnering with me in ministry and for making pastoral work satisfying. I am proud of you all.

ABOUT THE AUTHOR

Musa Bako is an executive coach and mentor. He holds a master's in coaching and mentoring from Sheffield Hallam University. Masters in theology from Crossroads Trinity Bible College and Theology, Manchester, UK. He was awarded an honorary Doctor of Theology degree from Crossroads Theological Seminary in Tallahassee, Florida, USA. He is the senior pastor of Victory Assembly (RCCG), a dynamic, growing, multicultural ministry through which God is impacting the people of Sheffield, United Kingdom, with the good news of Jesus.

Pastor Musa is also an assistant regional pastor within RCCG. He is a sought-after speaker at conferences and has spoken at conferences in Europe, Africa, the USA, and Canada. With the grace of God in his life and thirty years in pastoral ministry, Pastor Musa teaches the Word of God with maturity, clarity, and practical insight, helping people experience the life-transforming power of God for victorious living. His ministry thrust is to equip people with the tools to succeed in life and to fulfill the reason for which they were created. His messages and writings cut across cultural boundaries. Pastor Musa is married to Pastor Eunice Meque Bako, and together they are blessed with three children.

ABOUT THE BOOK

Satan and his demons are actively functioning in our world today, seeking to permeate every aspect of the human experience and rule in it. Satan has unleashed his demons on earth, and they are working aggressively to enthrone him as a god in the hearts of all people, in all nations, and have control over communities, villages, towns, and cities. Many of the events unfolding in the physical realm were initially determined in the spiritual realm.

This book is an attempt to expose the activities of the fallen Satan and his demons, their organized systems, their tools of operation, and the havoc they cause in the world. This book will equip the reader with tools to effectively defeat Satan and his demons and bring them into subjection as they journey through life to fulfil their destiny. I send out this book in prayer that the reader will become more aware of the spiritual forces in operation in his domain. I pray the reader will receive new power to function, no matter where their location is, and will go forward to enjoy victory in all spheres.

OTHER EXCITING BOOKS
FROM MUSA BAKO

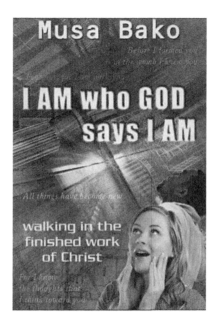

People come and go, but only a few people make a meaningful impact throughout their lifetime. Only a few people discover their purpose, turn it into passion, and fight for it like they don't have any other option. These are the people who reach greatness.

The vision of I Am Who God Says I Am is to demonstrate that you can achieve greatness in life and that there are no limitations before you.

ISBN: 978-88-89127-94-0

THE LOVE OF FATHER GOD

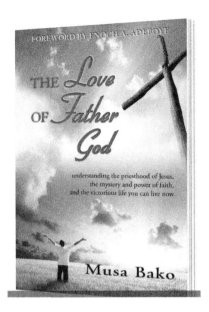

The Love of Father God unveils the heart and the never-ending love of God, the defeat and fall of Satan, and the power and glory of the Christian faith.

As a believer, you are a new creation in Jesus Christ—the wonder of God and the miracle of heaven. This book solves the mysteries and reveals the benefits of your role in God's kingdom.

ISBN: 978-88-96727-31-7

Destiny is within you are a proven guide that enables you to achieve the goals you set for yourself in life. You will discover that God created you for a specific purpose, and you exist to accomplish your God-given destiny.

You are not a loser, a burden, or a pest. You are a unique soul with special talents and gifts, and you can enjoy a wonderfully abundant life—no matter your background, education, or current economic situation.

ISBN: 9788897896289

Everybody Needs Somebody

Everybody Needs Somebody empowers you with tools to achieve a healthy and fruitful relationship in all spheres. There is something great in everyone—and yes, that includes you! Everybody has something to offer the world as a unique blessing.

ISBN: 978-1-4918-7516-2
ISBN:978-1-4918-7517-9

Lord, I Am Available; You Can Use Me

Lord, I Am Available; You Can Use Me is a handbook for men and women in ministry—those who are seeking to serve God effectively and influence their generation. God will use anyone and any situation to serve His purpose. He is the Creator of all things and Lord of all the earth; He can reach out, touch, and take anything He chooses to use, but not just anyone is given a righteous assignment. . .

ISBN: 978-1-5462-9362-0

Overcoming Discouragement

MUSA BAKO

Discouragement is a spirit that feeds on human tragedies, setbacks, unfulfilled expectations, and the uncertainty of life to ruin its victims. Discouragement can attack anyone, no matter how macho they may be—no matter how brave or educated they are or no matter what achievements they have made. The attack of discouragement is one of the reasons why many people cannot move forward in life; they cannot take the initiative to try something new. As a result of discouragement, many have dropped out of school, quit their job, closed their businesses, ended relationships, and walked away from ministry. This guide will help you combat the dangers of discouragement and forge a brand-new path!

ISBN 1728354978
ISBN 978-1728354972

OVERCOMING REJECTION

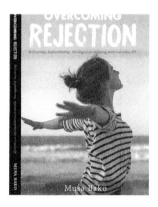

The author wrote Overcoming Rejection with three purposes in mind. Firstly, this book aims to provide readers with a deeper understanding of what rejection entails.

The purpose of this text is to explore rejection, including its root causes and the devastating impact it can have on individuals, in order to raise awareness and prevent others from inflicting it on anyone else. Secondly, to give tools to readers who are going through rejection and empower them to deal with it appropriately, overcoming adversity. Thirdly, to provide information and tools that will help people who are supporting others struggling with rejection.

Therefore, it is important that no one is made to feel unimportant in order for people to thrive and flourish in an environment of acceptance, love, and mutual respect. Nonetheless, rejection isn't something that anyone can completely avoid. We will all have to contend with it at some point but overcoming rejection will help you be prepared for truly anything!

ISBN:978-1685363475
ISBN: 1685363474

Stepping into God's promises for you

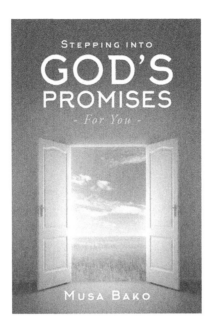

The inspiration behind 'stepping into God's promises for you' is to resource people with tools that can assist them in seeing God's word become a reality in their lives and situations. Everything written in the Scriptures is inspired by the Holy Spirit and can happen in anyone's life.

This book shows what God's promises are and what to do to make them happen. The promises in the scriptures, from Abraham to what is revealed in the epistles, apply to believers today. The new covenant is not lacking in any blessings of the Old Testament. New Testament believers enjoy a better and improved covenant.

ISBN: 13979-8888873915

Printed in Great Britain
by Amazon

45031605R00101